THE

BEST

AMERICAN

POETRY

1988

Dec 88

Happy birthday!

Happy

and la

love,

THE
BEST
AMERICAN
POETRY
1988

◇ ◇ ◇

John Ashbery, Editor

David Lehman, Series Editor

COLLIER BOOKS

MACMILLAN PUBLISHING COMPANY

NEW YORK

Collier Books
Macmillan Publishing Company
866 Third Avenue, New York, N.Y. 10022
Collier Macmillan Canada, Inc.

ISBN 0-02-044181-9
ISSN 1040-5763

Macmillan books are available at special discounts for bulk purchases
for sales promotions, premiums, fund-raising, or educational use.
For details, contact:
Special Sales Director
Macmillan Publishing Company
866 Third Avenue
New York, N.Y. 10022

10   9   8   7   6   5   4   3   2   1

Printed in the United States of America

CONTENTS

DAVID LEHMAN, poet and critic, has won numerous awards for his work, including The Paris Review*'s Bernard F. Conners Prize for 1987 and a National Endowment for the Arts fellowship grant the same year. He is the author of* An Alternative to Speech, *a poetry collection, and the editor of* Ecstatic Occasions, Expedient Forms: 65 Leading Contemporary Poets Select and Comment on Their Poems. *He writes for* Newsweek *and lives with his wife and son in Ithaca, New York.*

FOREWORD

by David Lehman

◇ ◇ ◇

The poet Don Marquis proposed a lovely simile for a perennial problem. "Publishing a volume of verse," he observed, "is like dropping a rose-petal down the Grand Canyon and waiting for the echo."

But bringing out a new poetry anthology—with plans to make it an annual event—isn't simply a quixotic gesture or a defiant one. It is also the product of a calculation. Given the popularity of creative writing programs in the United States today, isn't it reasonable to suppose that the potential audience for poetry is much wider than defeatists would think? There are annual anthologies devoted to the short story and there is one that selects among the year's best essays. Why not do the same with poetry, a genre of literature that continues to flourish despite unfavorable conditions? We might find that many readers are prepared to embrace contemporary poetry—if only a discriminating editor showed them what to look for.

That possibility is one of the reasons behind *The Best American Poetry*. A second is practical. Poetry of high quality is appearing in a dizzying range of publications; not even the most dedicated reader can keep up with it all. An annual anthology seems the obvious solution—so obvious that one wonders why it hasn't been tried before. There is certainly abundance enough to fuel a *Best American Poetry* annual, and make it live up to its name.

The basic idea is simple. Each year a different guest editor—a poet of distinguished stature—will select the poems and write an introduction to the volume. John Ashbery, the guest editor of our initial volume, helped me improvise the way toward a set of structural principles. I wanted to make sure that the guest editor would have maximum flexibility within defined limits. We decided that each year there will be no fewer than fifty poems and no more than seventy-five, that all selections will come from works published in the previous calendar year, and that no individual poet will be represented by more than three poems. Mr. Ashbery, who favors eclecticism and diversity as guiding virtues, chose seventy-five poems by as many different poets. It is entirely possible that next year's guest editor may, for example, settle on sixty poems—three by each of twenty poets.

Because audiences find helpful the incidental remarks that poets make between poems at poetry readings, I thought it might be interesting to try to produce a similar effect in an enlarged section of contributors' notes. Each poet was asked to write, in addition to biographical information, a comment on his or her poem—about its form or its occasion or the method of composition or any other feature worth remarking on. This was strictly optional; poets are entitled to their reticence. But I was pleased that so many took the time and trouble to meet my request. Their comments seemed invariably to enhance the pleasures of their work.

Other "rules" sound like compromises hammered out in congressional subcommittees. There was the question of sources. We elected to concentrate on magazines, big circulation periodicals as well as small press productions. But we stopped short of excluding books by individual poets. It is, after all, impossible to get a true measure of the state of contemporary poetry without appealing to poetry collections as well as to magazines. What about a poem that appeared in a magazine four years ago and was reprinted in a collection last year? To such questions, the anthologist's ever-ready response is: you just play it by ear.

Then there was the question of eligibility. How about foreign poets in residence in the United States or on long-term academic appointments at American universities? Did the "American" in our title have to mean "made in the U.S.A."? We worried about it but in the end decided it was foolish to be strict constructionists, especially in cases where the poet has come to seem a vital presence in a particular American community. Thus readers will note the work of John Ash and Seamus Heaney and Derek Walcott in this anthology. It, like Walt Whitman, is large enough to contradict itself with impunity.

As the series editor of *The Best American Poetry*, I have assigned a number of tasks to myself. In addition to maintaining continuity from year to year, enforcing such rules as there are, the series editor is expected to support and assist the guest editor, in part by scanning the world of magazines and making preliminary recommendations. But probably the series editor has no function more important than that of determining who the guest editor will be. I was lucky this year. John Ashbery is, in a phrase he once applied to Elizabeth Bishop, a "poet's poet's poet." It's irresistible to read over his shoulders, to get some sense of his taste and values and predilections. My thanks go to him; to my editor at Scribner's and Collier, John Glusman; and to a true friend of the project, Glen Hartley.

JOHN ASHBERY is best known as a poet but has also been active as an art critic, playwright, and translator from the French. Ashbery lived in France from 1955 to 1965, first as a Fulbright student and later as art critic for the International Herald Tribune. *He returned to New York in 1965 to become executive editor of* Art News, *a position he held until 1972. Since 1974 he has taught at Brooklyn College where he holds the rank of Distinguished Professor. He is the author of twelve books of poetry, including* April Galleons *(Viking, 1987). Twice named a Guggenheim Fellow, he received the Pulitzer Prize, the National Book Award, and the National Book Critics Circle Award for his 1975 collection* Self-Portrait in a Convex Mirror *(Viking). A volume of his art criticism,* Reported Sightings, *is to be published in 1989 by Knopf.*

INTRODUCTION

by John Ashbery

◊ ◊ ◊

One of the minor disadvantages of being a poet (as opposed to the major ones, which everybody—every poet at least—already knows about) is being continually asked who reads one's poetry. Or who reads poetry. This is annoying not so much because the question cannot be answered, but because the interrogator invariably assumes that the poet *must* know, with the implied assumption that if he doesn't there must be something wrong with him. Closely related to this question is another unanswered and unanswerable one: for whom do you write? Again the implication is that the writer of course knows, that any writer who doesn't ought to get out of the business of writing. There is a special anguish here for the poet: who wouldn't like to know for whom one is writing? If that were possible we could try to please them, tailor our writing not perhaps to their individual tastes but at any rate to a general profile of our actual and potential readers. Then they might like what we wrote; even critics might, and there would be an end to literary misunderstanding.

It never seems to occur to anyone that each reader is different, and that even those who might be said to resemble each other will each bring an individual set of experiences and references to their reading, and interpret and misinterpret it according to these. Alas, even to suggest that such a state of affairs exists is to invite further misunderstanding. It's no use trying, as I have done, to answer the question "For whom do you write?" with Gertrude Stein's brilliant, ask-a-simple-question-and-you-get-a-simple-answer formulation: "for myself and strangers." Like Cordelia's truthful answers, this one can infuriate the questioner, leading to charges of elitism, arrogance, and sedition.

Still another question that poets must be prepared for is some variation of: Is something happening in poetry today? Is poetry coming out of the closet, or the trunk? Why does it seem that people are suddenly bothering about poetry? Why am I asking you this question? Would you please account for the fact that your work interests me, perhaps only a very little but enough to make me curious about it? In the late 1950s my friend Frank O'Hara was invited for an after-work drink by a reporter from *Time* who cross-examined him in this fashion; O'Hara replied: "Sure there's something going on in poetry. Otherwise you wouldn't be buying me this drink." As far as I know, *Time* didn't print that.

After more than forty years of observation, I have come to the conclusion that there is always something happening in poetry, but it always seems as though it had just begun to happen. The main difference between then and now is quantity or volume: there are more places for poets to publish, hence more poets and poems— or does it work the other way round? And poets are certainly more visible now. In the forties there were few poetry readings, with only a handful of elder statesmen of poetry ever called upon to read in public. Probably the Beat generation changed all that: poets, a few of them at least, performed in public and became celebrities, and then others, not necessarily media material, joined their ranks, and suddenly in the larger cities there were readings in bookstores and churches and cafés almost every night. This happened when I was out of the country; returning to New York from France in 1963 for a visit after an absence of five years I was startled when asked to give a reading, and more surprised to discover how commonplace such events had become. And the poetry-reading industry continues to thrive. Poets are no longer faceless; many have become public figures, of a sort, and they are expected to perform. After every reading members of the audience come forward with copies of the poets' books for them to autograph. It's not even always a book—sometimes it's a photocopy of a poem from a magazine or even a paper napkin. On one occasion a man asked me to autograph a book which, it turned out, I had already autographed for him at a previous reading. When I pointed this out, he asked me to sign it with a fresh autograph. And recently in Washington, D.C., I was approached after a reading by a young man who said he was on a limited income and had already bought a book last week when another poet had been there, and would I please autograph it? It turned out to be Allen Ginsberg's *White Shroud*. When I balked at autographing someone else's book, he became so insistent that I finally did sign my name on the back endpaper, leaving the flyleaf for Allen to sign should he pass through Washington again.

Even taking the ordinary zaniness of American life into account, such occurrences can stir up suspicions about the so-called poetry revival: once again, *is* something happening in poetry? Or is it only one more fad in a series of so many in our history? Are these fans merely the avatars of those who mobbed Jenny Lind and Oscar Wilde when they toured the country, and promptly forgot about them the next day? Poetry publications abound, stacks of books are sold after readings, but does anyone read them? Or are they meant never to be opened, like the limp-leather volumes of Emerson's essays and *Lalla Rookh* that adorned "library tables" in thousands of American homes at the turn of the century?

More to the point, do even poets read poetry? Having taught writing classes for quite a few years, I have my doubts. The reading lists I give out seldom get examined very closely. Frequently when I tell a student that, on the basis of his work, he must have been reading William Carlos Williams recently (or Pound or Moore or Bishop or Auden), I am met with a blank stare: the student has not read the poet he seems influenced by, has perhaps not even heard of him, but like an unwitting version of Borges' Pierre Ménard, has produced his own *Don Quixote* while remaining uncorrupted by knowledge of the original.

But I don't wish to belittle students: how many "mature" poets read each other's work? I have to confess to some laziness in this regard, and therefore can't really condemn the writing student who wants to be heard without listening to others. I hasten to add that I am perhaps an extreme case: I know scholar-poets who manage to "keep up" with the bewildering proliferation of contemporary poetry; people like John Hollander or Richard Howard or the late Robert Duncan, whose knowledge of poetry is encyclopedic, who live and breathe poetry every day and in whom poetry begets poetry. But what of the others? Many, perhaps the majority, respond to other stimuli which also result in poetry: poets who mostly listen to music or look at movies or pore over newspapers or travel literature or scientific journals (as Marianne Moore did), or who perhaps do not much of anything but write poetry. Is their poetry any better or worse because of this? Certainly one wouldn't have wished Miss Moore to have proceeded otherwise, given the results, nor wished Dr. Williams away from his patients or Wallace Stevens from the offices of the Hartford Insurance Company. Who knows, perhaps they would have been better if circumstances had allowed them to keep their noses permanently "stuck in a book," but in the absence of proof to the contrary let's settle for them as they are.

Yet it can do no harm for us poets to come to know each other's work. Reading through the poetry of 1987 I was struck, perhaps for the first time, by the exciting diversity of American poetry *right now,* and by the validity of this diversity, the tremendous power it could have for enriching our lives—I hesitated before using this hoary phrase but am going to let it stand. And what a pity that so few of us avail ourselves of it. For I think that even the most literate of readers of American poetry tend to confine themselves to a narrow segment of it. In traveling around the country I have noticed that the landscape of American poetry is strangely fragmented and gerrymandered; its partisans frequently blinkered. It is odd that in the age of the global village, a quaint regionalism stubbornly prevails. In New York, audiences like to listen to poetry of the New York School; the spirits of Frost and Lowell are alive and well in New England; in Tennessee, poetry other than that of Tate and Warren is viewed with suspicion; in the Pacific Northwest it is felt that poetry should be modeled after that of Roethke and William Stafford—two poets who, except for that accident of geography, would not seem to have much in common. Further down the coast one can almost hear the assertive voices of Duncan and Rexroth speaking out of the San Francisco fog. And of course Olson, who turns up elsewhere as well, as do the relatively recent Language Poets (no one seems to be able to define this term, so I won't try), many of them based in southern California, though they have chapters in Michigan, New England, and New York. Otherwise the reasonable voices of the writers associated with the Iowa Writers Workshop have the Midwest pretty much to themselves—except for a Chicago-style funk which turns up both in poetry and the visual arts.

Instead of congratulating ourselves on so much diversity we tend, as so often in America, to choose up sides and ignore anyone not on our team, much as "single-issue" voters choose their political candidates. At the risk of producing cacophony, I have tried to bring together a number of poets of different persuasions in this anthology. I like things that seem to me good of their kind, and don't especially care what the kind is. I have enjoyed juxtaposing poets as unlike each other as Richard Wilbur and Kenward Elmslie, Joseph Brodsky and Kenneth Koch; young, unknown poets (at least they were to me) like Joe Ross and Lydia Tomkiw with established ones like Donald Hall and Donald Justice. I have some prejudices: there is not much "political" poetry that I like, for the reason that the political sentiments reiterated in it are usually the exact ones I already harbor, and I would rather learn something new. Still, there are exceptions to this rule as to every other, and politics in the poems by Alan Williamson, Wanda Coleman, and Philip Levine reprinted here sounds fresh and newly minted to me.

I like the light these poets involuntarily shed on each other. I think we read them differently in such mixed company, where they are inflected by the tuning-fork vibrations of their neighbors. Leafing through this anthology one can be reminded that red looks very different when placed next to green; that a d-sharp and an e-flat sound different in different contexts. One doesn't approach an anthology in the same way one approaches a collection of poems by a single poet: in the former case a "rubbing off" happens that can be disorienting but—I hope—also stimulating, and of course we can always return to our favorite poets for more concentrated scrutiny on some other occasion.

In discussing the supposed gulf between abstract and representational art, the late French painter Jean Hélion wrote in his journal: "I wonder . . . whether all the valid painting being done today doesn't bear certain resemblances which escape us at the present time." One could wonder the same thing about poetry, but in the meantime, while we await that uniform utopia, the dissimilarities —the splintering, the impurity—could be those of life itself. Life is what present American poetry gets to seem more like, and the more angles we choose to view it from, the more its amazing accidental abundance imposes itself.

THE
BEST
AMERICAN
POETRY
1988

◇ ◇ ◇

A. R. AMMONS

Motion Which Disestablishes Organizes Everything

◇ ◇ ◇

William James (*The Varieties of Religious Experience*, p. 84) is
   to be
commended for penning out of our finest recommendations
   for the bright outlook:

he was so miserable himself he knew how to put a fine
   point on the exact
prescription: he knew that anybody who knows anything
   about human

existence knows it can be heavy: in fact, it can be so
   heavy it can undo
its own heaviness, the knees can crumple, the breath
   and heart beat,

not to mention the bowels, can become irregular, etc.: but
   the world,
William knew, sardonic and skeptical, can characterize
   sufferers of such

symptoms malingering wimps, a heaviness not to be
   welcomed by a person who
like me feels like one of those: weight begets weight and
   nature works as well

(and mindlessly) down as up: you have to put English of
   your own into
the act misleading the way into lightenings: brightness,
   however

desirable, is a losing battle, though, and James knew it can
   be depended on
more often than not that folks won't have spare
   brightnesses on them every

morning that they want your heaviness to cost them: so, in
   general, if
someone asks how you are, no matter how you are, say
   something nice: say,

"fine," or "marvelous morning," and, this way, hell
   gradually notches up
toward paradise, a misconstruction many conspire to
   forward because

nearly all, maybe all, prefer one to the other: oppositions
   make things costly:
crooked teeth encourage the symmetry of braces but as
   soon as everybody's

teeth are perfect, crooked teeth misalign: something is
   always working
the other way: if you let the other way go, you get more in
   Dutch for

while the other way at first may constitute an alternative
   mainstream,
pretty soon it breaks up into dispersive tributaries and
   splinters a

rondure of fine points into branches and brooklets till it
   becomes
impossible to get a hold on it, a river system running
   backwards:

be bright: that is a wish that can be stable: you can always
   think of
happiness because it's wished right out of any rubbings
   with reality, so

you can keep the picture pure and steady: I always imagine
   a hillock,
about as much as I can get up these days, with a lovely
   shade tree and under

the tree this beautiful girl, unnervingly young, who
   projects golden
worlds: this scene attracts me so much that even though
   I'm a little

scared by it it feels enlivening, a rosy, sweet enlivening:
   poets
can always prevent our hubris, reminding us how the
   coffin slats peel

cloth and crack in, how the onset of time strikes at birth,
   how love falters,
how past the past is, how the eyes of hungry children feed
   the flies.

from *The Hudson Review*

Shadow Play

◇ ◇ ◇

She leaves the motor running.
I would too. I would like to marry her, that face
repeated a million times in this town.
In the exhaust next door a man
twists his wooden leg into an impossible
position. He doesn't even have to say
"I know, I know, and nobody resents me."
He just grins.

On the vendor's tin scales, daylight
shifts and splinters. Blood on the black brick,
a shopkeeper sweeps glass from his eyelids.
A young man fidgets in a doorway,
cups his hand around a blue
flicker of panic, and leans back
into the shuffling papers and footsteps,
the noise that opens away from him
and is not noise.

Now a cleaning lady stops herself
and looks over her shoulder. And so does
the mailman, a traffic cop, a kid walking his bike.
And the perfect word lodges
deep in the throats of businessmen
talking gibberish, drawing lines around themselves
until obsessed and hailing taxis.
Only our loose clothes

between us, the linen tablecloths, white
as blindness. Only the putter of canal boats,
the vine-covered walls, some cursory
glance that empties our eyes, when they meet,
of options, and won't let go.
A person who might

grow older. People who will dash their dreams.
People who will come back and
live in the aroma of bread, in the sound of
a thousand doves unfolding the plaza.
I would like a glass of ice water.
It's the little thing, when I'm lucky
the world comes to me.

from *Poetry*

Bases

◇ ◇ ◇

Birds in flight switch places above and below a hypothetical bar—
like a visual trill—though imitation is vulgar.

The idea that each individual is a unique strain: weight and counter-
weight in the organization of memory. So many forms represent-
ing, presumably, a few wishes.

Chew the fat in order to spill the milk, in other words, from which
the self-same woman emerges.

What the cool tomato cubes forming a rosette around this central
olive have to do with love and happiness.

Thrilled to elaborate some striking variant of what we imagine to
be a general, if fabricated, condition.

Two men on the street wax their teal-green, '50s Mercury.

She thinks the two are lovers, but you say you disagree. Now she's
angry either because you mimic, or because you merely mimic,
ignorance of such things.

She uses intercourse to symbolize persuasion.

Old people never appear to have reserved judgment in the manner
of a poised beauty.

She dreamed the ill were allowed to wander at ease through the reconstructed, but vacant, Indian village.

Her eyes scanning the near range with a feeble sense of their being like children sledding, though never having done that adds a campiness to the "Whoo-ee" of "I see."

You're not crying because you can't find the thing you made, but because she won't help. She won't because she's comfortable, reading—but not really because now you've stuck your head behind her shoulder sobbing and pretending to gasp. She goes away to pick up your clothes, but also to see if she can find the thing you want. You tell her it looks like a crab. While she's gone you find it underneath her chair. You insist, bitterly, that you knew where it was all along; you were just testing her ability to see. It's like keeping her eye on a bouncing dot. She says either you're lying now or you were lying before when you were sobbing for it and needed her help. Really she thinks you were lying both times, all along, but not exactly.

Now the news is of polls which measure our reactions to duplicity.

She puts her tongue to the small hole, imitating accuracy.

from *O.blēk*

Memories of Italy

◇ ◇ ◇

for Pat Steir

I loved the light of course
and the way the young men
flirted with each other.
I loved the light,—

the way it fell out of a sky like a painting,
or perhaps like the ground (if this
is not too paradoxical a way of
putting it) for a painting,

and the way the young men stood in the station
wearing jeans that were the colour of the sky
or the sea in a painting, jeans that revealed
the shapes of their legs which reminded me

of the statues in the square outside the station
where the light fell with such violence
their shadows were blacker than the despair of the painter
who cannot proceed with the painting: the canvas
is before him, its ground blue and blank as the sky above the station

where the young men loiter like the heroes in one of the lulls of
     the Trojan War
when lazy picnics were possible beside the calm sea, under the
     smiling sky,

and it half seems that the war will end forever, for surely they
   must all soon fall in love with each other . . .
And the painter knows his painting must be heroic, that the blue
   is not the sky
but a terrible sea a God has raised to drown the beauty of the
   young men in the marble battlefield of the station,

and he knows the painting is finished,
that it represents the envy the divine must feel
towards the human as marble must envy the sea,

and the painting is hung in the concourse of the station
and the young men drift indifferently to and fro before it:
their feet hardly seem to touch the blue marble ground.

      from *Disbelief*

JOHN ASHBERY

One Coat of Paint

◇   ◇   ◇

We will all have to just hang on for awhile,
It seems, now. This could mean "early retirement"
For some, if only for an afternoon of pottering around
Buying shoelaces and the like. Or it could mean a spell
In some enchanter's cave, after several centuries of which
You wake up curiously refreshed, eager to get back
To the crossword puzzle, only no one knows your name
Or who you are, really, or cares much either. To seduce
A fact into becoming an object, a pleasing one, with some
Kind of esthetic quality, which would also add to the store
Of knowledge and even extend through several strata
Of history, like a pin through a cracked wrist-bone,
Connecting these in such a dynamic way that one would be forced
To acknowledge a new kind of superiority without which the world
Could no longer conduct its business, even simple stuff like
     bringing
Water home from wells, coals to hearths, would of course be
An optimal form of it but in any case the thing's got to
Come into being, something has to happen, or all
We'll have left is disagreements, *désagréments*, to name a few.
Oh don't you see how necessary it is to be around,
To be ferried from here to that near, smiling shore
And back again into the arms of those that love us,
Not many, but of such infinite, superior sweetness
That their lie is for us and it becomes stained, encrusted,

Finally gilded in some exasperating way that turns it
To a truth plus something, delicate and dismal as a star,
Cautious as a drop of milk, so that they let us
Get away with it, some do at any rate?

from *Shenandoah*

TED BERRIGAN

My Autobiography

◇ ◇ ◇

For love of Megan I danced all night,
fell down, and broke my leg in two places.
I didn't want to go to the doctor.
Felt like a goddam fool, that's why.
But Megan got on the phone, called
my mother. Told her, Dick's broken
his leg, & he won't go to the doctor!
Put him on the phone, said my mother.
Dickie, she said, you get yourself
up to the doctor right this minute!
Awwww, Ma, I said. All right, Ma.
Now I've got a cast on my leg from
hip to toe, and I lie in bed all day
and think. God, how I love that girl!

from *New American Writing*

Chinese Space

◊ ◊ ◊

First there is the gate from the street, then some flowers inside
    the wall,
then the inner, roofed gate. It is a very plain wall, without
    expressionistic means,
such as contrasting light on paving stones inside the courtyard to
    the calligraphed foundation stones.
My grandfather called this the façade or Baroque experience,
    rendering a courtyard transparent.
The eye expecting to confront static space experiences a lavish range
    of optical events,
such as crickets in Ming jars, their syncopation like the right, then
    left, then right progress
into the house, an experience that cannot be sustained in
    consciousness, because
your movement itself binds passing time, more than entering
    directs it.

A red door lies on a golden mirror with the fascinating solidity and
    peacefulness of the pond
in the courtyard, a featureless space of infinite depth where neither
    unwanted spirits nor light
could enter directly from outside. It lies within the equally whole
    space of the yard
the way we surrounded our individuals, surrounded by a house we
    could not wholly
retain in memory. Walking from the inner gate across a bridge
    which crossed four ways

over the carp moat, turning right before the ice rink, we pass roses
   imported from Boston,
and enter the main courtyard, an open structure like a ruin. This is
   not remembering,
but thinking its presence around eccentric details such as a blue and
   white urn turned up to dry,
although certain brightnesses contain space, the way white
   slipcovered chairs with blue seams
contain it.

The potential of becoming great of the space is proportional to its
   distance away from us,
a negative perspective, the way the far corner of the pond becomes
   a corner again as we approach
on the diagonal, which had been a vanishing point. The
   grandmother poses beside rose bushes.
That is to say, a weary and perplexing quality of the rough wall
   behind her gives a power of tolerance
beyond the margins of the photograph. Space without expansion,
   compactness without restriction
make this peculiar and intense account of the separable person from
   her place in time,
although many families live in the partitioned house now. The
   reflecting surface of the pond
would theoretically manifest too many beings to claim her particular
   status in the space,
such as a tigerskin in space.

After the house was electrically wired in the thirties, he installed a
   ticker tape machine connected
to the American Stock Exchange. Any existence occupies time, he
   would say in the Chinese version,
reading stock quotations and meaning the simplicity of the courtyard
   into a lavish biosphere,
elevating the fact of its placement to one of our occupation of it,
   including the macaw speaking Chinese
stones representing infinity in the garden. This is how the world
   appears when the person

becomes sufficient, i.e., like home, an alternation of fatigue and
    relief in the flexible shade of date trees,
making the house part of a channel in space, which had been
    interior, with mundane fixtures
as on elevator doors in a hotel, a standing ashtray that is black
    and white.
The family poses in front of the hotel, both self-knowing and
    knowing others at the same time.
This is so, because human memory as a part of unfinished nature
    is provided
for the experience of your unfinished existence.

from *Conjunctions*

Noch Einmal, an Orpheus

◇ ◇ ◇

When the Queen of Darkness heard his voice,
That mortal stranger, saw him lift the lyre
And watched the dull throng of the dead rejoice
To hear him tell of earth and earth's desire,
Of pain, of longing, she was not amused.
She caught that veiled allusion to the shame
Of her own story and would have refused
Him then and there, had not the shades that came
In droves now clamored so for his request.
"Be rid of him," she breathed to the immense
Stillness at her side, who thought it best
To play a cruel joke at the man's expense,
Fated as he was to indecision,
To second thoughts, a lifetime of revision.

from *Grand Street*

Momentariness

◇ ◇ ◇

It is conceivable that when one dies
if one has leisure, realizing, suddenly, remembering
that now there will be no one that will know one at some given
     moment, see
or hear one, listen to
one's voice, one will discover, looking back
whom formerly, if anyone, one loved,
identifying them (in retrospect) by one's remembrance of some
     satisfaction
at something one had said to them—at having said it—
that seemed to one informative, that is,
an indication of oneself within the range of reason
& observation: as though—we know there is no bridge—
across the pillars of the bridge there isn't one had jumped, delivered
the letter, returned & now again was standing on the other side
& felt that one had managed to put aside, in stealth, a little of
     oneself
in trust which time now on its visits could not get at,
search as it might one's person: it was gone.
The other had it.
The selfish chance to make these dubious gifts of knowledge of
     oneself
is lost at death.

To have space means to extend, and perhaps to move, to have
place around one, defended or
desired. You can stretch,
having lain down
can get up.

And perhaps walk some distance.

Space stretches, extension, in all directions from any point
at all times unaltered.

The calculations of the engineers to whom sunlight moves
        notwithstanding,
it is the shadow of perspective of the hypothetical eye, the sheer
possibility of your movement onward, time
permitting, your time. Could a man aging at an extremely low rate
        of speed
move straight (as they say: straight) onward forever?

from *Tyuonyi*

JOSEPH BRODSKY

To Urania

◊ ◊ ◊

I.K.

Everything has its limit, including sorrow.
A windowpane stalls a stare; nor does a grill abandon
a leaf. One may rattle the keys, gurgling down a swallow.
Loneliness cubes a man at random.
A camel sniffs at the rail with a resentful nostril;
a perspective cuts emptiness deep and even.
And what is space anyway if not the
body's absence at every given
point? That's why Urania's older than sister Clio!
In daylight or with the soot-rich lantern,
you see the globe's pate free of any bio,
you see she hides nothing, unlike the latter.
There they are, blueberry-laden forests,
rivers where the folk with bare hands catch sturgeon
or the towns in whose soggy phonebooks
you are starring no longer. Further eastward, surge on
brown mountain ranges; wild mares carousing
in tall sedge; the cheekbones get yellower
as they turn numerous. And still further east, steam
   dreadnoughts or cruisers,
and the expanse grows blue like laced underwear.

from *The Paris Review*

21

Miranda in Reno

◇ ◇ ◇

In a silent room surrounded by sand I sleep.
Sometimes the phantoms of the dead
on the far shore wrestle for hours
with the great questions he and I—
and everyone we had ever forgotten—
abandoned when we fell out of love,
when the long nights appropriated us.

Or maybe they aren't phantoms.
It's winter on that island, the frozen
snow is bricked high for miles,
like a seawall to discourage visitors:
in spring it will thaw, the beach will flood,
and the actors masquerading as ghosts will drown.

To marry means to halve one's rights & double one's duty.
Or as a friend observed at his ex-wife's wedding:
divorces open out, marriages close in.
Really both are imaginary lines over which
two briefly parallel lines intersect,
creating a rectangle—a cell.
Everyone I know is drowning trying to escape some island.

Other times, the dead on their milky shore
rock in unison in marble chairs
and agree that the great questions
were so many distractions they erected
like a long white wall to keep themselves
from falling too deeply in love.

Last night in the dry stillness I dreamt
of that island again: the snow fell fast
and under the ice the drowned men recited
their lines, scripted subtly by my former husband.
It's true, you see, they aren't phantoms.
But who can say how I came to this desert,
all my lights burning at noon, and the phone—
off the hook for days—ringing again.

from *The New Republic*

Mecox Road

◇ · ◇ · ◇

for Darragh Park

An American friend using a thick British accent,
said I looked rather pensive that day,
but there was nothing to report from the front,
no need to test the waters or repent.
The preoccupation, quite insurgent,
quite maniacal, was with a wooden bench.

You can see it from the porch,
the porch that like the house, was built in 1912.
Its pale, grey tone, its flaky skin,
the used feeling of its slats formed by wood and air,
invite the inviting emptiness of an inanimate object,
compared to the fact that there's room
on the bench for two or three people.

There's a white wicker rocking chair on the porch.
I sat down on it. My early years had been
filled with dreams of white columns,
and there they were, bracing the roof of the porch,
its ceiling painted blue.
Did you know that flies can distinguish color?
The blue color keeps the flies
from getting too bold, even when someone's flesh
might seduce them into a false confidence or real urge.
The area is patrolled by color.

So it's just a nice coincidence that the blue ceiling
turns out to be pleasing.
What if black was the color that kept them at bay?
Next time I walk into your studio,
I'll watch the flies react to the colors in your paintings.
Yesterday I had the urge to walk inside
the depths of those paintings,
and leave the past behind forever.

Still, being who I am, the bench preoccupied me.
It sits near to the pond,
and appears rather stately and majestic.
It seems to say, "It's good to be king."
That very seat has the power to move nations to violence,
and the wisdom to bring about a resounding peace.
A pond is a quiet thing. This particular pond is man-made.
The anti-fly blue is rich, soft and milky.
Imagine the bench bedecked with the crown jewels.

Black-eyed Susans and many other flowers
whose names I do not know,
help to form the mowed paths
that correspond to a way of getting to
the bench and to the pond.
Some of the flowers have been growing wild there for ages,
and some were planted by the painter.
It's hard to get lost along those paths,
but one can still maintain the regard for choice,
and a natural curiosity. From these paths,
one can see the backside frame of the house.
"Simple as how they used to do it,"
is a large part of any beauty.
As we take the time to observe, the sun and shadows
set the table for dinner. If there's a morality play here,
it's that the bench could be a pregnant house,
as well as a casket. There's room for a proud father
and mother to think about the dead fathers and mothers.

There's room for the fruits of action and inaction,
and the grey areas of indecision and noninvolvement
that help color the black suits.

Two lives could reach an agreement while sitting on
that bench, two lives with very different needs,
very different philosophies and ways of expressing
the same independent thing.
Two lives could meet here like anywhere else,
and for a moment be concerned with the same thing.
Now the king and queen of the bench are nothing
more than ghosts who can no longer remember the names
of the countries that flanked their borders,
or recall the names of their rivals.
Sometimes the royal couple feels that this is good.
They watch the painter who bought the old bench
walk the paths with his dog Oriane.

Monkeys could be wild in those trees, rabbits
roam the grounds. They watch him stop here and there
to observe and touch, to feel and see
just what paintings might be growing there
as the heart of the day is concealed from the night.
And now the haunted rulers of the bench
declare the bench holy and divine, and promise
to defend the honor of the bench, even if
that defense means war. They call on the poets
to praise the would-be soldiers, not knowing
that this praise can no longer exist.
While they drink from their goblets,
Oriane spots a small rabbit. Before disappearing,
they call out, "Same time, same place, next year."
The sun and shadows disappear,
and the rabbit spots Oriane and races for the brush.

It starts to rain, and no one has any protection.
The sun has a coat, the moon has a cape.
There's a wonderful willow

in the field between the porch and bench,
it's very feminine. His own judge and jury are naked,
the accused are all blind.
Mecox Road has become a summer shortcut,
interrupting a world that encourages fantasy,
a world that depresses with its mere possibility.
We build something from this, particularly
when we are strong. The passing cars can be seen
and heard from the porch. They become part of
a diary that moves clockwise and counterclockwise,
like the history of the beach where the drivers
and passengers arrive to and leave from.
They usually leave with more color in their faces,
and sometimes the sunburn can be chilling.

Eventually, you'll only hear the cars from the porch.
The trees will take care of that, monkeys or not.
Just like you insured that Oriane will live
for the rest of Man's life, there may be a fire,
and everything that has appeared to be true,
even history, may be burned.
By then, the bench might have a bidet next to it,
or maybe the bench will be struck by lightning
and broken in half. Perhaps some next generation owner
will remove it altogether unless the land becomes
museum grounds, and the house becomes a museum.

This is what I'm betting on. The flowers are trite
and engaging, the property is as charming
as a man or a woman can be.
Though tomorrow has nothing to do with today,
the bench's pep talk incorporates the past,
and is exhilarating. I asked if nature can be
soothing, and the answer was yes,
until you know that it is or isn't there.
I think, and therefore I hope that whoever
lives on this land when the trees have ruined
the view of the road, will be as lucky as we are today,

and will not have to rely on four-leaf clovers.
By then, religion and blasphemy could be the same thing,
splitting the common wind like an axe to a tree.
Barring disease, the lone white birch
will continue to stick out from the rest.

The rusted wheelbarrow is turned upside down.
Still being who I am, I'm glad the painter
doesn't use it much. More depends on color than dirt,
more depends on a watery footprint than its representation
cast in mud. Without the dream of possibility,
there is no love. Sorry Freud, there are such things
as accidents. Love is an accident waiting
to happen. Maybe history is everything that was never
said or told, everything that was always hidden.
It happened by the bench. The pond was sleeping,
and at another point, design entered into the picture.
The bench knows that well.

Other owners might have planted corn and potatoes,
now wild berries are the only edible things that grow here.
We imitate the rain and try to flood the night
with a few substitute colors. Some are invited,
some just drop in. The very texture of escape is impossible.
A man who just died appears on a canvas in the studio.
He is wearing a pair of red pants.
The landscape is a bare room where there is
no simple answer to the mysterious question,
"Where does the split occur?"

The bench asks that we hold fast
to our history, the pale, grey chores that invent plans
and surprises for the normal and neurotic, and for those
who are different. Everything here is more sacred than
civilization, but everything here is very civil.
The rainwater that winter turns into snow
reminds us that we must do more than plant
and eat the harvest. The landscape will be covered with

a blanket that he didn't ask for. The slatted seat,
buried under a white confluence of everything that has fallen,
will survive the next coldness and accept the glad offerings
that wait a few months down the road.
Hold on to your hat. Even if the bench is left
unprotected like ourselves, and disintegrates into nothing
like a blessing or a sin, he can still sell his soul
while he watches the fish swim at the springtime edge
of the pond. The man-made pond is his harvest.

A blunt, human memory, forgetful of events,
and glad to be so, will have a place to take its vows
when the springtime coughs up the ghosts
that have slept all winter. It could have happened here,
or it could be natural enough to happen here.
There will be a dog to lick your feet,
but no one can predict whether the house and bench
will still be here. The pale, grey wood is less
and more of what it isn't. It's a blind and most
beautiful child, and you'll be able to decide
whether to look at it or not, whether to sit down near it
or touch its warm flesh, and by then
we'll be mourning the death of the snow.

from *Verse*

WANDA COLEMAN

Essay on Language

◇ ◇ ◇

who stole the cookie from the
cookie jar?

this began somewhere

   suggest middle passage. consider the dutch ship
   consider adam and eve and pinchmenot

blacks think in circles she said. no they don't
i said it too readily, too much on the defense. of course
blacks think in circles. i think in circles
why did i feel it necessary to jump on the defensive.
   defensiveness
is sure sign of being gored by unpleasant truth

equation: black skin + new money = counterfeit

i keep going back over the same thoughts all the time (the
   maze
   poverty poverty poverty
syndrome oft times accompanies social stigmata)
   sex sex sex
desperately seeking absolute understanding (the way out)—
   black black black
the impossible (my love relationship wears me thin) i know

number one stole the cookie

but knowing doesn't
stop me from thinking about it—trying to be the
best i can spurred by blackness but they keep telling me the
best fashion in which to escape linguistic ghettoization
is to
ignore the actuality of blackness blah blah blah and it will
cease to
have factual power over my life. which doesn't
make sense to me—especially when the nature of mirrors
is to reflect

when a mirror does not reflect what it is? not necessarily a
    window,
merely glass? can it be something other than a glass? and once
it becomes glass can it ever be a mirror again?

    violent animal can't take it no more can't
    take it anymore from anyone tired of being
    one in a world of everybodies and someones
    violent animal you throw chalk against the
    blackboard rocks at reluctant lovers assault
    money-grubbing landladies with cold dishwater
    they're all against you in that paranoiac $$$
    prism keep trying to see yourself/reflection
    oooh black as swamp bottom mired in muck you
    violent animal struggle struggle struggle to
    get to solid ground get free get solidified/

    grounded

substitute writer for mirror, visionary for window, hack for
    glass

who me? couldn't be

(smashing is addictive and leads to greater acts of violence/
throwing things, i.e. the first sign of danger)

equation: colorlessness + glibness = success

i am occasionally capable of linear thought, stream of
    consciousness
and hallucinate after a three day fast (have eyes will see)

i'm much too much into my head. stressed. i can't feel
anything
below the neck

                                        number two stole the cookie

he says he hates me
and i'm wondering what in
hell on earth did i do except
be who he says he loves to hate

equation: circle + spear = spiral

going down and in at the same time going outward and up

absolutely

this ends and begins here

                from *Heavy Daughter Blues*

A Monologue

◇ ◇ ◇

What did I say? What did I say?
I could tell you what's going on. What it
means but not all of it. Just a lot.
A lot doesn't mean much. It's whatever
I can stand or not. I can't remember.
What's the good of it. Nobody . . . The last time I . . .
There's nobody here of course. Not a bit of it.
Lots of it went away, by, came loose, went past,
gone away, not bad. Necessarily. They tell you
things but you don't remember them.
There's something they could tell you if they would
but it wouldn't stand. Lingering. To linger
is not to stay exactly. Stay what? I can't
think what exactly. I could try to remember
to think of what to tell you and then it wouldn't
be so hard to stay here. Without.

There's the evidence. It was passed off by
somebody as a black maul. Passed. A passing
fancy that in time may. But open
the question with a deterrent. Like me.
I'd never pass judgement on the here today done
again tomorrow. You like it and it has you.
Smile. Talk about. See to it that the cables
all appropriate. Joining in takes a lot of solace.
You see them about it and they tell you to wait too.
They're a margin, marginal, tangent to the main

ounce. I'd like to put something by me.
Something for a late month. The time the sun
turned out a ton all broadcast. They couldn't
all find out to take in. Not even the wheat.
Rows and rows. Sandwiched between and now
and again a sort of strain. The moon will
not train. We're not solved to entertain.
We're to keep to ourselves and I'd say so surely too.

Night. It's always open in this place.
Closed in spaces all up in a shovel scatter.
Books, the andirons left a space for, or moths.
Let's have a notion and build from there.
You'd carry anything with little strain, less decision,
if you had the memory. The likeness.
Duckpins blow over in yellow pools of torch.
And I told him then, I said the man without
assignment must stand in the rain. Without
spoil. Now the tar gets to leak from the
battery last beam up to the left. The notion
that's not worth its shoe leaves its slots for
departures. Nice to pretend in this last
light out the walking hour. Demand of the
little import it be stated.

Got to bend in the basement most dictionary place.
Possible to have it be aporia near Peoria?
A quiver. Night raisin the dogs bring me and stop
signs. Get rid of these words and not hoping see
them thin into place without plan. A voice
does not terrace its ends. Stop theater,
ceasing volume, raging stun. The mother, the mother
of the child rhyme, sunset sign not enter into it.
Pedal out of breath. I live near this moon
by the house.

A broad dry thudding winter with the clouds
cladding down. I haven't been able to see it.
I've had to make away. To settle up the bill.
To stand in a hill until the sands remake.
I don't know. I do what's nearly already made.
No expectations on a corner lot. They've all
come down, sated among. Then the light's fluid
flashes in the frame. Words like brads lined up.
You take them down, settle them. Apparent, this.
No mug would parry. I half way enjoy it,
take a scad or two. Before the horizon.
Before the sun. In a lamp's nick. I could
have made it all up before but I had the
miles on dwindling.

It leads me into a world of strangeness,
everytime I open a lick, a statutory lick.
Beyond intent, more than I thought, beyond
what I had to say, but never what I meant
to have. The world came around on me again.
This chair squeaks, when I move only slightly.
I hadn't thought it to be in need of a touch.
I thought to wait. I thought to myself.
I thought to pass but I never thought it.
When you think to say it you better mean it, none of
this turning out the same. Passing all right.
Passing failure.

A world all out of streamers, you say you
think? None of it. A stegosaurus on a
windowsill, brass, morning sun, collected. I walk
down the hall and turn back, my thought won't
hold me. I'd have to measure myself back
from the first one. I'd have to erect
great sand corridors in imagination and
turn them down. Half-light, storms in
the evening, expectable stiff interruptions.
I'll show you what it's like, half-hoping I

won't have to. I have my pride, I have
my eyes, the first thing you notice, the last
one to go. There it stands, the monument
to daylight, heading straight along the horizon in
the window frame. And at night savages,
fitting appointments, ruby running lights.

Actually it's not a matter of the cup's being on top
of the other cup. Actually it's a matter of
the putting away. An awful horn went off.
My chair. The putting away is a matter of
knowing without thinking where things go.
The things fly from your hands into their slots.
It's so right. You don't have to think of
anyone deciding, though it's your wife did once.
No doubt. Stillness of things entering their
places. You, an agent. And then you stretch
out your arms to as far as they go and nothing
more needs a touch. It's right.
What's that on the stove? And so still
you miss the pleasure.

There are diamonds under the ground. I
think about them. Then I go flying.
I reach out my hands and there's nothing there.
Wonder. To be the agent of absence.
You're solid, of absolutely no standing at all.
Mistless. Thoughtless. Where is the mistress?
The mattress? The longings and more or less
the short of it? All gone down and out over.
Diminishless widening thrall without the plummet.
But without the plummet where are we?
Nice today. Tourniquet. Shelf. Amalgam.

I could live better if you would move over.
We could share. The ointment is on the ledge.
These are my chairs. The ones with the seat back.
And the elms, no caring for them, the windows
enough. You sit by one. Put your hands where
I wish. Do the same to you. Thoughts of
a vintage, a quietness same. I am as
able as you'd give me leave. I am as stable.
There are oranges under the table. We never
ate in those days. We shared a common fear.
Muttering. Rather the screams. What about
the Arab tribes? The marshmallow bill?
The weighted planks? What if I wrote
this all out? What would it take me?
How would you take me? The olives
that rolled down the tube and plunged into the fire.
The oxcart wreck you wanted a picture of.
I remember too much. And you too.
We start out along the walls, the stuff, the beds.
We are consumed.

A man needs. I hate that stuff,
it screws your mind four ways from winter.
I don't want the people here, the persons,
the friends. Let them make their fly-bys
out on their limbs. I mean to be
incarcerated. This writing sealed in limedwell.
There is a mystery that must be preserved.
I must live to hear the words. I will not speak.

from *O.blēk*

New Year

◇ ◇ ◇

Another year, another return—
Each one has drawn closer to home.
A perennial naif, whose pleased
intake of breath is meant to welcome
back the urban crush, prefers

familiar brickfronts and squares
even to vistas down the proud
colonnades and quays of Paris,
mountains lost among high clouds,
or domes at dawn in the pastel east.

These westward windows, fifteenth floor,
make a triptych frame for sunset—
which shows the buildings as somehow more
thoughtful than they often get
described as being; while the sky,

with blue impartiality,
may be forecasting the first
snowfall. . . . To sense purpose in turning
to the desk again seems right,
the crossed-out sentences and lines

summoning words and pauses always
nearer those that will be felt
as having stood by from the start,
waiting to assume their place.
The heat clicks on. Somewhere a bell. . . .

All the objects here have twinned themselves
with stories. The room's a cradle, or an ark;
it says that half the point of our departure
is coming back—suggestion followed by one
who breaks off work to watch the setting sun.

from *Partisan Review*

Dog Star Sale

◊ ◊ ◊

Now the universe wants to be known for
Itself, isn't that why we're here
Popped out on this terrace the color of stars
The red ones like gentrified brick

Lucky for us
It takes money to even imagine
Such things and this, for parsecs around
Is the one place where money is made
Though not everyone has it, not even here
The burden is on those who do
Which we freely take up
A volitional duty to curate the spheres
After how many misfired suns
And misapplied genes
How many millions fed to despair
Before we were brought to the task
Thankless, that cannot be failed

Just to think of it
Sometimes engenders a chill
So thorough the planet's own breath
Will draw back on its bones
And there in that vault sucked by fear
One has shivered at twinkles of something
Not normally shown. It explains
The wide pupils and why I protect them

When doing so keeps me from you
All involved on the earth with your chores
Of pollution and likely never to pause
Let alone practice
What we've observed: as far as you touch
Other worlds, that much you save yours

from *The Paris Review*

The Dream

◇　◇　◇

What you think you
eat at some table like
a pig with people
you don't even

know and lady there
feeds you all and you,
finally you at least
are full, say, look at

them still eating!　Why
(says a woman, another
sitting next to me) those
others still eating you

so cannily observed are
unlike you who *could* be fed
because you were hungry!　But
them, they can't—they

are possessed by the
idea of hunger, *never* enough
to eat for them, agh . . .
Or you either, dreamer,

who tells this simple
story being all these
same offensive persons
in one empty head.

from *Exquisite Corpse*

TOM DISCH

In Memoriam

◇ ◇ ◇

Nothing, no one, gives me rest
I have put it to the test
And it is not an idle jest
The life I live must lead to death
An emptiness and end of breath
Though still my heart beats in my breast
Nothing, no one, gives me rest

The streets are filled with cryers crying
No end of them, nor yet of dying
Some men may smile a little while
If sellers sell and some are buying
But they will join the rank and file
Who decorate our ancient Nile
No end of them, nor yet of dying

Memorials are built and then
Time silts a harbor, forms a fen
And tells its immemorial jest
To the worst as to the best
The world will be as it has been
I am feeling so depressed
Nothing, no one, gives me rest

from *Boulevard*

Top O' Silo

◇ ◇ ◇

On summer evenings, the main event in Aberdeen, S.D., back a good ways, was the swift passage through town of the crack Great Northern and Pacific streamliner, *The Rocket*. Five minutes of binocular time could be had for a nickel, on the observation deck above Top O' Silo, a bar and grill which *was* on top of a silo, catercorner from the train station. Pointing up to its row of lit windows, spit 'n' whittlers, on their bench in front of Tiny's Cafe, would josh strangers looking for its whereabouts, "If it was a diamondhead rattler, you'd be a goner."

The height of Top O' Silo varied with the seasons and the harvests. It could be raised or lowered, like a cumbersome elevator, by an electric microdrive system invented and patented by its owner-manager, Zeke Spink. The metal hull of the silo could be opened at various points to provide windows. The view was nothing to write home about in late winter, or, if the crops failed, in summer and fall. As the fodder underneath was depleted, the row of lit windows would sink down to tree level. Most years, Top O' Silo pressed down upon a fulsome cargo, rye and alfalfa and barley, harvested in abundance, the pressure serving a utilitarian purpose highly regarded in the community, hastening the process that creates sweet silage. The resulting heat kept Top O' Silo snug, in summer too, when dusks turned chill. When the silo was full, the bar and grill offered an ideal vantage point from which to survey Aberdeen and environs: the railway yard, tracks fanning out in all directions across prairie, more prairie, still more prairie, the enveloping flatness rendering the details of the town all the more precious—even the glum foundries and machine shops, the squat pork-packing factory with its burning hair aroma, and, dominant though shuttered, the opera house with its twin onion towers of silvery tin, fronting onto a small park graced by a cluster of stunted Russian olive trees, roots fed by Moccasin Creek, not deep enough to wet a man's privates, so the spit 'n' whittlers proclaimed, not that they'd ever put this handed-down bit of lore to the test.

Young rowdies, Rocket Racketeers they called themselves, would gather at Top O' Silo, having given their home-cooked suppers time to settle, and pick a number out of Zeke's white Stetson planted next to the register, by the toothpick glass. The winner, highest number, got to plunk a nickel into the one binocular viewer, having climbed a considerable distance in drought years, up to the observation deck. At the first sound of a wail, in the nickel would go, and the binocular viewer would be swerved east, as far as it would go, to catch the approach of the red snout ripsnorting its way west, straight as an arrow, crossing *Les Mauvaises Terres* by midnight, on to Butte, Boise, Seattle, perdition and paradise, past homesteads and sister silos, approaching Aberdeen only to vanish momentarily behind the crenellated sanatorium of Dr. Hudson, eminent specialist in tumor disease, renowned for employing chemical coagulation of his own invention in preference to the knife or radium, more toots, the speed-demon snout would reappear, cut off from its body by Dr. Hudson's parapets, conjoined again, then, like a serpent representing Evil in a political cartoon, split into bits and pieces by houses and stores and churches, then the disappearance behind the station, not slowing down one iota, emerging again, snout now lost from sight, west, west, hurtling past a landscape with few ideas, coaches and pullman cars to be counted, the dining car casting slanty yellow patches on the darkening mauve of the flatlands, more pullmans, the lounge car bringing up the rear, the backs of heads lined up, ladies with white hats on, indoors, and the last of it, the observation platform, striped awning overhead, two deck chairs, a couple, the man gets up, moves behind the woman, adjusts her white wrap so it hangs evenly over her shoulders, a sweater with long sleeves that dangle limply, angora most likely, expensive and soft to the touch, fending off the chill, his hands caress her shoulders, she reaches up, her hand is on his hand, guiding it, under the angora.

The questions heat up at Top O' Silo. What were the family of four eating? The little girl in yellow taffeta was having grape Jell-O. The others were digging into pie à la mode. When the darky brought them coffee, the little girl held up her cup. The old woman slapped her wrist and the girl began to cry. What was the name of the dining car? Lake of Galilee. Was it crowded? Packed, every seat taken, people waiting in line. And the lounge car. Millard Fillmore. Always is, Mondays, Wednesdays, Fridays. White hats? Six. Yesterday it was only four. The record stands at twelve, last August. Cal saw fifteen, fifth of July. He's no respecter of truth. He is when it comes to brand names. Price tags. He fudges on price tags since he stopped seeing Jeanette. He's no respecter of truth. He is when it comes to what time it is. The argument is a distraction from nightfall. And the couple? He went inside. She sat there awhile, knitting. Then the little girl and the old woman came out and stood at the rail. The old woman opened her handbag and gave the little girl a stick of gum. The little girl unwrapped the stick of gum and wadded the tinfoil into a ball. Then she threw it over the railing. The old woman slapped her wrist. The girl began to cry. The woman in the deck chair folded her knitting away and got up and went inside. What did you say the family of four were eating? Grape Jell-O and pie à la mode. And the lounge car. Millard Fillmore. But today's Thursday. So it is. Somebody screwed up. Without *The Rocket*, there'd be less to pick over. A sandlot. Patches of grass. The alfalfa underneath, heating up to make sweet silage for the hogs for the pork-packing factory. Is this all there is to life? That's a big question, unspoken at closing time.

from *Conjunctions*

Losing It

◇ ◇ ◇

You feel a hardcore blankness
gain the upper hand
while the world turns to glittering
silica, crinkles and rolls
up like a rented movie screen.
The air whirrs: surely
the golden fan that halos saints' heads,
electric and on high,
is rising from your spine.
Before your lips hit the floor
you recognize divestment
and want to dicker, please heaven,
with the slippage, but find yourself
dismissed. Getting lost

was once adventure. As a kid
you and a kindly aunt played at it,
boarding any bus that puffed along, no matter
where it went. Your aunt was mindful
of the transfers, which saw you home
intact. Where is she now
with her calm tokens and cerebral maps?
When your brain's become a Byzantine cathedral

flooded with the stuff of sump and dumpster.
Its frescoes, memories, confetti
into the mortal sludge.
From domes filleted and boned
with light, the impounded soul looks down.

You wake up dumb
as something fallen off a turnip truck
into a new Dark Age. That petrified
river round your legs must be your skirt.
What month? What day? the doctor asks.
Mortified, you lug the answer, a book
dense as a headstone, to your lips.
"I don't know," you whisper.

If brain were body
yours would be unmuscled
and standing in the buff.
The ooze of stupefaction
extends for blocks,
and you have nothing
but a cotton swab
with which to mop it up.
Above the bed, like a sylph
in a filmy sarong,
his head on a plate
of light, Christ sinks
into a blue plush cross.
Pain was never so fey.
Heroic, yet decorative,
he is the way
we wish death to be.
How well he embodies our need
for pleasantry. The oxygen is delicious
as champagne. You wish
to express this dim epiphany.
You'd like to
binge on the fidgety past,

but thoughts sigh slow as elevators
from cell to cell.
And words . . . words are snow
crystals to be grown from vapor.

Outside, the setting sun
dips a straw into the trees
and drinks their green.
This time you are lucky.
You've lost nothing
to speak of: a contact, a way of seeing.

Thinking back on what happened, you imagine
the brain as Byzantine cathedral, flooded
with the stuff of sump and dumpster.
Its frescoes, memories,
confetti into the mortal
sludge. From domes filleted
and boned with light, the impounded soul
looks down.

Then you discard the flood,
which was a kind of comfort; let go
the pan-religious romance of the soul.
What's left—a state
that's strictly ex- and un-,
not-this, not-that, the ne
plus ultra of losing
track: A nothing so engulfing
I had to hide behind
the second person to address it,
as though I spoke of someone

else. I remember my mother
folding my aunt's best blue pajamas
on the empty drawer of her
dresser in intensive care.
If there's a soul it's such

a clingy rayon casing,
deflating almost to absence
when creased in layers of tissue.
From the high ground of health
and self-control, I issued orders to
Try. Her lids, pinned by ether,
strained as she complied.
Squeezing a hand I hadn't
held since childhood, I wanted to forget
myself and beg her to awaken.
Come back, no matter
where you're headed,
the voice inside me said.

from *Epoch*

Marriage

◇ ◇ ◇

Romance is a world, tiny and curved, reflected in a spoon. Perilous as a clean sheet of paper. Why begin? Why sully and crumple a perfectly good surface? Lots of reasons. Sensuality, need for relief, curiosity. Or it's your mission. You could blame the mating instinct: a squat little god carved from shit-colored wood. NO NO NO. It's not dirty. The plight of desire, a longing to consort, to dally, bend over, lose yourself; be rubbed till you're shiny as a new minted utensil. A monogrammed butter knife, modern pattern or heirloom. It's a time of plagues and lapses, rips in the ozone layer's bridal veil. One must take comfort in whatever lap one can. He wanted her to bite him, lightly. She wanted to drink a quart of water and get to bed early. Now that's what I call an exciting date. In the voodoo religion, believers can marry their gods. Some nuns wed Jesus, but they have to cut off all their hair first. He's afraid he'll tangle in it, trip and fall. Be laid low. Get lost. Your face, lovely and rough as a gravestone. I kiss it. I do.

In a more pragmatic age many brides' veils later served as their burying shrouds. After they'd paid their dues to mother nature, they commanded last respects. Wreaths, incense and satin in crypts. In India marriage of children is common. An army of those who died young march through your studio this afternoon to rebuke you for closing your eyes to the fullness of the world. But when they get close enough to read what's written on your forehead, they realize you only did what was necessary. Then they hurriedly skip outside to bless your car, your mangy lawn and the silver floss tree which bows down in your front yard.

His waiting room is full of pious heathens and the pastor calls them into his office for counseling, two by two. Once you caressed me in a restaurant by poking me with a fork. In those days, any embrace was a strain. In the picture in this encyclopedia, the oriental bride's headdress looks like a paper boat. The caption says "Marriage in Japan is a formal, solemn ceremony." O bride fed and bedded down on a sea of dexatrim, tea, rice and quinine, can you guide me? Is the current swift? Is there a bridge? What does this old fraction add up to: you over me? Mr. Numerator on top of Miss Denominator? The two of us divided by a line from a psalm, a differing line of thinking, the thin bloodness line of your lips pressed together. At the end of the service guests often toss rice or old shoes. You had a close shave, handsome. Almost knocked unconscious by a flying army boot, while your friends continued to converse nonchalantly under the canopy of mosquito netting. You never recognized me, darling, but I knew you right away. I know my fate when I see it. But it's bad luck to lay eyes on each other before the appropriate moment. So look away. Even from this distance, and the chasm is widening, the room grows huge, I kiss your old and new wounds. I kiss you. I do.

from *New American Writing*

On Difficulty

◇ ◇ ◇

It's that they want to know *whose* they are,
seen from above in the half burnt-out half blossomed-out
woods, late April, unsure as to whether to
turn back.
The woods are not their home.
The blossoming is not their home. Whatever's back there
is not. Something floats in the air all round them
as if *it* were the place
where the day drowns,
and the place at the edge of cries, for instance, that fissure, gleams.
Now he's holding his hand out.
Is there a hollow she's the shape of?
And in their temples a thrumming like
what-have-I-done?—but not yet a question, really, not
yet what slips free of the voice to float like a brackish foam
on emptiness—
Oh you will come to it, you two down there
where the vines begin, you will come to it,
the thing towards which you reason, the place where the flotsam
of the meanings is put down
and the shore
holds. They're thinking *we must have slept a while,*
what is it has changed? They're thinking
how low the bushes are, after all, how finite
the options one finds in the
waiting (after all). More like the branchings of whiteness
always stopping short into this shade or that,

breaking inertia then stopping,
breaking the current at last into shape but then
stopping—
If you asked them, where they first find the edges of each other's
        bodies, *where*
happiness resides they'd look up through the gap
in the greenery you're looking down through.
What they want to know—the icons silent in the shut church (to
        the left),
the distance silent in the view (to the right)—
is how to give themselves *away,*
which is why they look up now,
which is why they'll touch each other now (for your
looking), which is why they want to know what this
reminds you of
looking up, reaching each other for you to see, for you to see by,
        the long sleep
beginning, the long sleep of resemblance,
touching each other further for you that Eternity begin, there,
        between you,
letting the short jabs of grass hold them up for you to count by,
to color the scene into the believable by,
letting the thousands of individual blossoms add up
and almost (touching her further) block your view of them—
When you look away
who will they be dear god and what?

from *The End of Beauty*

Snow White and Rose Red

◇　◇　◇

The bear at the door, begging
to be beaten free of his snowy coat,
was a king's son under a curse,
detail my sister and I learned long after

we scoured him with brooms and then lay down,
pale crescents pinned to his vast dark.
Rose claimed that in firelight
his fur glittered, but I saw no more

than before, when a coin warmed in my hand
pressed a queen's profile into the ice
grown in fronds against the window.
In the eye-size opening melted tear by cool tear,

had I seen something break from the forest's deep ranks?
I saw nothing beyond an animal knowing—
if it be knowing—what a lost hunter does:
on such a night any warmth will do.

So in the heart of a wood a man will sleep
inside the beast he's slain, waiting daybreak
to illumine the way toward any clearing.
Toward a cottage like the one where red roses

and white clambered to the window,
the sanguine and the snowflake's distant kin
spendthrift with promise of good company
as they vied for my sister's shears.

In a cut-glass vase too fine for the rough table
on which lay bread and books for two,
a bouquet would hold its salon
while as always we rudely, mutely read—

Rose, someone's travels bound in red morocco;
I, botany for the season ahead,
where "naked" meant "without specialized scales,"
and "tender": "not enduring winter,"

the author looking out for those
after his own heart: "If it is too cold
to read in the field, save this
for the warmth of home."

Shadows unroll across the bluing snow
but enough oblique light has pierced
a man-made pond gracing the palace grounds
that, out of a slow, internal melting,

ice crystals regrow into bloom and thorn
as men harvest them, sawing the water
into frozen bales, loading sledges
tomorrow will drag to the icehouse.

The tree overlooking this—is it weeping?
Not markedly weeping.
Are the leaf scars solitary?
There are two or more at each node.

The bear, that long-lost night?
He was one of two brothers.
One picked Rose to wed,
the one who had been animal chose me.

Wind rattles a fist of milkweed
until it's prised open, loosing a handful
of tufted ha'pennies one by one,
that each be borne far off and root where it falls.

from *The New Yorker*

The Piano Player Explains Himself

◇ ◇ ◇

When the corpse revived at the funeral,
The outraged mourners killed it; and the soul
Of the revenant passed into the body
Of the poet because it had more to say.
He sat down at the piano no one could play
Called Messiah, or The Regulator of the World,
Which had stood for fifty years, to my knowledge,
Beneath a painting of a red-haired woman
In a loose gown with one bared breast, and played
A posthumous work of the composer S——
About the impotence of God (I believe)
Who has no power not to create everything.
It was the Autumn of the year and wet,
When the music started. The musician was
Skillful but the Messiah was out of tune
And bent the time and the tone. For a long hour
The poet played The Regulator of the World
As the spirit prompted, and entered upon
The pathways of His power—while the mourners
Stood with slow blood on their hands
Astonished by the weird processional
And the undertaker figured his bill.
—We have in mind an unplayed instrument
Which stands apart in a memorial air
Where the room darkens toward its inmost wall

And a lady hangs in her autumnal hair
At evening of the November rains; and winds
Sublime out of the North, and North by West,
Are sowing from the death-sack of the seed
The burden of her cloudy hip. Behold,
I send the demon I know to relieve your need,
An imperfect player at the perfect instrument
Who takes in hand The Regulator of the World
To keep the splendor from destroying us.
Lady! The last virtuoso of the composer S——
Darkens your parlor with the music of the Law.
When I was green and blossomed in the Spring
I was mute wood. Now I am dead I sing.

from *Grand Street*

Words

◊ ◊ ◊

The simple contact with a wooden spoon and the word
recovered itself, began to spread as grass, forced
as it lay sprawling to consider the monument where
patience looked at grief, where warfare ceased,
eyes curled outside themes to search the paper
now gleaming and potent, wise and resilient, word
entered its continent eager to find another as
capable as a thorn. The nearest possession would
house them both, they being then two might glide
into this house and presently create a rather larger
mansion filled with spoons and condiments, gracious
as a newly laid table where related objects might gather
to enjoy the interplay of gravity upon facetious hints,
the chocolate dish presuming an endowment, the ladle
of galactic rhythm primed as a relish dish, curved
knives, finger bowls, morsel carriages words might
choose and savor before swallowing so much was the
sumptuousness and substance of a rented house where words
placed dressing gowns as rosemary entered their scent
percipient as elder branches in the night where words
gathered, warped, then straightened, marking new wands.

from *Tyuonyi*

Nourishment

◇ ◇ ◇

Love—its long spoon, its promise, and its threat—
you won't go empty, I shall make you eat,
  I'll fend off death—
apostrophizes an averted face,
retreats with a reluctant backward glance.

Agitated wings
flap at the cold containment of the moon,
  fluttering
batlike, bewildered out of a dark cave,
and bump themselves on light's solidity

as on an arm outstretched in utter trust,
patient as trees, pouring itself until,
  ethereal,
it has been drained of every precious cell
to share with who may happen to be dry.

A house of appetite and sustenance
links, shelters, and divides
  inhabitants who feed,
work, walk together and as in a dream
undoing the loose bonds of need float free.

You and I, walking toward this silent house,
encounter no warm gold
    ring of lantern light
such as draws chilly travellers and moths.
No lamp burns here but blood,

mortal fuel consumed at steady speed.
Ghosts in disappointment flit away,
    hunger unsatisfied.
Dim in the room we turn to one another,
open our lips, and speak

a single word and raise a mutual finger.
Into such stillness no new thing should spill,
    muddy the mirror
we turn our double back to speechlessly
and sit and eat our fill.

from *Boulevard*

DONALD HALL

Prophecy

◇ ◇ ◇

I will strike down wooden houses; I will burn aluminum
clapboard skin; I will strike down garages
where crimson Toyotas sleep side by side; I will explode
palaces of gold, silver, and alabaster:—the summer
great house and its folly together. Where shopping malls
spread plywood and plaster out, and roadhouses
serve steak and potatoskins beside Alaska King Crab;
where triangular flags proclaim tribes of identical campers;
where airplanes nose to tail exhale kerosene,
weeds and ashes will drowse in continual twilight.

I reject the old house and the new car; I reject
Tory and Whig together; I reject the argument
that modesty of ambition is sensible because the bigger
they are the harder they fall; I reject Waterford;
I reject the five-and-dime; I reject Romulus and Remus;
I reject Martha's Vineyard and the slamdunk contest;
I reject leaded panes; I reject the appointment made
at the tennis net or on the seventeenth green; I reject
the Professional Bowling Tour; I reject matchboxes;
I reject purple bathrooms with purple soap in them.

Men who lie awake worrying about taxes, vomiting
at dawn, whose hands shake as they administer Valium,—
skin will peel from the meat of their thighs.
Armies that march all day with elephants past pyramids
and roll pulling missiles past Generals weary of saluting

64

and past President-Emperors splendid in cloth-of-gold,—
soft rumps of armies will dissipate in rain. Where square
miles of corn waver in Minnesota, where tobacco ripens
in Carolina and apples in New Hampshire, where wheat
turns Kansas green, where pulpmills stink in Oregon,

dust will blow in the darkness and cactus die
before it flowers. Where skiers wait for chairlifts,
wearing money, low raspberries will part rib-bones.
Where the drive-in church raises a chromium cross,
dandelions and milkweed will straggle through blacktop.
I will strike from the ocean with waves afire;
I will strike from the hill with rainclouds of lava;
I will strike from darkened air
with melanoma in the shape of decorative hexagonals.
I will strike down embezzlers and eaters of snails.

I reject Japanese smoked oysters, potted chrysanthemums
allowed to die, Tupperware parties, Ronald McDonald,
Karposi's sarcoma, the Taj Mahal, holsteins wearing
electronic necklaces, the Algonquin, Tunisian aqueducts,
Phi Beta Kappa keys, the Hyatt Embarcadero, carpenters
jogging on the median, and betrayal that engorges
the corrupt heart longing for criminal surrender:
I reject shadows in the corner of the atrium
where Phyllis or Phoebe speaks with Billy or Marc
who says that afternoons are best although not reliable.

Your children will wander looting the shopping malls
for forty years, suffering for your idleness,
until the last dwarf body rots in a parking lot.
I will strike down lobbies and restaurants in motels
carpeted with shaggy petrochemicals
from Maine to Hilton Head, from the Skagit to Tucson.
I will strike down hanggliders, wiry adventurous boys;
their thighbones will snap, their brains
slide from their skulls. I will strike down
families cooking wildboar in New Mexico backyards.

Then landscape will clutter with incapable machinery,
acres of vacant airplanes and schoolbuses, ploughs
with seedlings sprouting and turning brown through colters.
Unlettered dwarves will burrow for warmth and shelter
in the caves of dynamos and Plymouths, dying
of old age at seventeen. Tribes wandering
in the wilderness of their ignorant desolation,
who suffer from your idleness, will burn your illuminated
missals to warm their rickety bodies.
Terrorists assemble plutonium because you are idle

and industrious. The whip-poor-will shrivels and the pickerel
chokes under the government of self-love. Vacancy burns
air so that you strangle without oxygen like rats
in a biologist's bell jar. The living god sharpens
the scythe of my prophecy to strike down red poppies
and blue cornflowers. When priests and policemen
strike my body's match, Jehovah will flame out;
Jehovah will suck air from the vents of bombshelters.
Therefore let the Buick swell until it explodes;
therefore let anorexia starve and bulimia engorge.

When Elzira leaves the house wearing her tennis dress
and drives her black Porsche to meet Abraham,
quarrels, returns to husband and children, and sobs
alseep, drunk, unable to choose among them,—
lawns and carpets will turn into tar together
with lovers, husbands, and children.
Fat will boil in the sacs of children's clear skin.
I will strike down the nations, astronauts and judges;
I will strike down Babylon, I will strike acrobats,
I will strike algae and the white birches.

Because Professors of Law teach ethics in dumbshow,
let the Colonel become President; because Chief Executive
Officers and Commissars collect down for pillows,
let the injustice of cities burn city and suburb;
let the countryside burn; let the pineforests of Maine

explode like a kitchenmatch and the Book of Kells turn
ash in a microsecond; let oxen and athletes
flash into grease:—I return to Appalachian rocks;
I shall eat bread; I shall prophesy through millennia
of Jehovah's day until the sky reddens over cities:

Then houses will burn, even houses of alabaster;
the sky will disappear like a scroll rolled up
and hidden in a cave from the industries of idleness.
Mountains will erupt and vanish, becoming deserts,
and the sea wash over the sea's lost islands
and the earth split open like a corpse's gassy
stomach and the sun turn as black as a widow's skirt
and the full moon grow red with blood swollen inside it
and stars fall from the sky like wind-blown apples,—
while Babylon's managers burn in the rage of the Lamb.

from *The Paris Review*

Thin Air

◇　◇　◇

What if I did not mention death to get started
or how love fails in our well-meaning hands
or what my parents in the innocence of their malice
toward each other did to me. What if I let the light
pour down on the mountain meadow, mule ears
dry already in the August heat, and the sweet
heavy scent of sage rising into it, marrying
what light it can, a wartime marriage,
summer is brief in these mountains, the
ticker tape parade of snow will bury it
in no time, in the excess the world gives
up there, and down here, you want snow? you think
you have seen infinity watching the sky shuffle
the pink cards of thirty thousand flamingos
on the Serengeti Plain? this is my blush,
she said, turning toward you, eyes downcast
demurely, a small smile playing at her mouth,
playing what? house, playing I am the sister
and author of your sorrow, playing the Lord
God loves the green earth and I am a nun
of his Visitations, you want snow, I'll give you
snow, she said, this is my flamingos-in-migration
blush. Winter will bury it. You had better
sleep through that cold, or sleep in a solitary bed
in a city where the stone glistens darkly
in the morning rain, you are allowed a comforter,
silky in texture though it must be blue,

and you can listen to music in the morning,
the notes nervous as light reflected in a fountain,
and you can drink your one cup of fragrant tea
and rinse the cup and sweep your room and
the sadness you are fighting off while the gulls'
calls beat about the church towers out the window
and you smell the salt smell of the sea
is the dream you don't remember of the meadow
sleeping under fifteen feet of snow though you half
recall the tracks of some mid-sized animal,
a small fox or a large hare, and the deadly
silence, and the blinded-eye gray of the winter sky:
it is sleeping, the meadow, don't wake it.
You have to go to the bottom of the raveling.
The surgical pan, and the pump, and the bits
of life that didn't take floating in the smell
of alcohol, or the old man in the bed spitting up
black blood like milk of the other world, or the way
middle-aged women from poorer countries are the ones
who clean up after and throw the underwear away.
Hang on to the luxury of the way she used
to turn to you, don't abandon it, summer
is short, no one ever told you differently,
this is a good parade, this is the small hotel,
the boathouse on the dock, and the moon thin,
just silvering above the pines, and you are starting
to sweat now, having turned north out of the meadow
and begun the ascent up granite and through buckthorn
to the falls. There is a fine film on your warm skin
that you notice. You are water, light and water and thin air,
and you're breathing deeply now—a little dead marmot
like a rag of auburn hair swarms with ants beside the trail—
and you can hear the rush of water in the distance
as it takes its leap into the air and falls. In the winter
city she is walking toward you or away from you,
the fog condensing and dripping from the parapets
of old apartments and from the memory of intimate garments
that dried on the balcony in summer, even in the spring.

Do you understand? You can brew your one cup of tea
and you can drink it, the leaves were grown in Ceylon,
the plump young man who packed it was impatient,
he is waiting for news of a scholarship to Utrecht,
he is pretty sure he will rot in this lousy place
if he doesn't get it. You can savor the last sip
and rinse the cup and put it on the shelf
and then you go outside or you sit down at the desk.
You go into yourself, the sage scent rising in the heat.

from *Antaeus*

SEAMUS HEANEY

A Shooting Script

◇　◇　◇

They are riding away from whatever might have been
Towards what will never be, in a held shot:
Teachers on bicycles, saluting native speakers,
Treading the nineteen-twenties like the future.

Still pedalling out at the end of the lens,
Not getting anywhere and not getting away.
Mix to fuchsia that "follows the language."
A long soundless sequence. Pan and fade.

Then voices over, in different Irishes,
Discussing translation jobs and rates per line;
Like nineteenth century milestones in grass verges,
Occurrence of names like R. M. Ballantyne.

A close-up on the cat's eye of a button
Pulling back wide to the cape of a soutane,
Biretta, Roman collar, Adam's apple.
Freeze his blank face. Let the credits run

And just when it looks as if it is all over—
Tracking shots of a long wave up a strand
That breaks towards the point of a stick writing and writing
Words in the old script in the running sand.

from *American Poetry Review*

Envoi

◇ ◇ ◇

A voice that seems to come from outer space,
Small, Japanese (perhaps the pilot of
One of these frisbee saucer flights that trace
Piss-elegant trajectories above

Sharp eyes and index-finger landing pads)
Speaks to me only with its one-watt tweeter
(A dodderer among these dancy lads)
And firmly orders: "Take me to your reader."

My Muse. I'd know her anywhere. It's true
I'm no Bob Dylan, but I've more than one
Electric fan who likes the things I do:
Putting some English on the words I've spun

And sent careening over stands of birch
To beat the local birds at their own game
Of taking off and coasting in to perch,
Even, perhaps, in pigeon-cotes of fame.

They are my chosen envoys to the vast
Black Forests of Orion and The Bear,
Posterity's faint echo of its past,
And payload lifted into haloed air.

from *The Yale Review*

The Confessions of Gerrit

◇ ◇ ◇

I drink a lot of skimmed milk.
I use Lysol Spray in the bathroom.
I stare long and hard at pretty faces.
I'm afraid to ask for the real price of my work.
I write poems, high, after midnight, *well* after.

I stay home alone on Saturday nights.
I have laid in a good supply of Tucks.
I've gotten fat to ward off AIDS.
I've used diet pills to help me work—and think.
I don't exercise anymore, except coming up the stairs.

I was bored by *A Clockwork Orange*, the movie.
I pore over the *National Enquirer*.
I've read about 30 pages of Proust's novel(s).
I like Peggy Lee better than Ella Fitzgerald.
Doesn't that say something awful about me?

My parlor palm is dying, frond by yellowing frond.
I think I'm running out of things to confess.
I'm no Augustine, or even Christina Crawford.
I usually feel like an ass-hole.
I say "Hi, guys!" to dogs tethered on the street.

I write art criticism faster than I can read it.
I don't always enjoy Henry James.
Maybe Geraldine Page is my favorite movie star,
If I could just think of a few movies she starred in.
I hope I am very ambitious.

from *Mudfish Two*

JOHN HOLLANDER

An Old Story Is Retold

◇ ◇ ◇

Great, dark wings, passing my roof over
Confound, rather than reassure:
What am I left with to endure?
What love will forty years recover?

The primal steps of freedom pound
Across the dry floor of the deep
In annual echo now, the sleep
Of exile cushioning the sound;

And the long march through wilderness
And out and into wild once more,
The olive leaves of each new shore
Spelling out writs of dispossess.

Our own diasporas begin
With first steps toward a rising sun,
Shading themselves, before they've done,
Conducting their own evening in.

May we live past this winter, then
When harps are cold and fingers numb,
Jerusalemed, the year to come,
In one another's arms again.

from *Partisan Review*

The Foreigner Remembered
by a Local Man

◇ ◇ ◇

Fuseli! I fancied the floor would tumble down—
could he be less than a giant, genius itself?
Footsteps approached, then a bony little hand

slid round the doorframe, followed presently
by a lion-faced, white-haired pygmy of a man
in a gown of old flannel gathered round his waist

by a length of rope, and wearing on his head
what I made out with some surprise to be
the bottom of Mrs. Fuseli's sewing basket . . .

My work was there. The Maestro stared about.
"By Godde," said he, "you will nefer paint finer.
It vas alvays in you, I haff said, and now,

by Godde, it is out! You haff de touch—it is
Wenetian entirely. But you look demn tin."
To such a point our converse fired him up

we drove instanter to Park Lane, the while
he swore like a fury—a very little one—
yet how relentless was his vehemence

as he strode among the marbles, filled with zeal:
"De Greeks vere goddes, goddes vere dey." It proved
a scene immortal in my sanguine life . . .

So far from London's smoke offending me,
it has always seemed sublime, a canopy
shrouding the City of the World. "By Godde,"

Fuseli said as we took the air that day,
"it is de smoke of Israelites making bricks."
"Grander, sir," said I: "it is the smoke

of a people who in freedom would have forced
the Egyptians rather to make bricks for them."
"Vell done, John Bull!" Fuseli cried aloud.

And now, this morning, Reynolds came: "He's gone."
"Who, sir?" "Fuseli." "A man of Genius . . ." "But
I fear of no principle." "Why, sir, say you so?"

"He has left, I hear, such drawings—quantities
shockingly indelicate." I had no heart
to finish my figure. Today must be a blank.

from *For Nelson Mandela*

Nostalgia of the Lakefronts

◇ ◇ ◇

Cities burn behind us; the lake glitters.
A tall loudspeaker is announcing prizes;
Another, by the lake, the times of cruises.
Childhood, once vast with terrors and surprises,
Is fading to a landscape deep with distance—
And always the sad piano in the distance,

Faintly in the distance, a ghostly tinkling
(O indecipherable blurred harmonies)
Or some far horn repeating over water
Its high lost note, cut loose from all harmonies.
At such times, wakeful, a child will dream the world,
And this is the world we run to from the world.

Or the two worlds come together and are one
On dark sweet afternoons of storm and of rain,
And stereopticons brought out and dusted,
Stacks of old *Geographics*, or, through the rain,
A mad wet dash to the local movie palace
And the shriek, perhaps, of Kane's white cockatoo.
(Would this have been summer, 1942?)

By June the city seems to grow neurotic.
But lakes are good all summer for reflection,
And ours is famed among painters for its blues,
Yet not entirely sad, upon reflection.
Why sad at all? Is their wish not unique—
To anthropomorphize the inanimate
With a love that masquerades as pure technique?

O art and the child are innocent together!
But landscapes grow abstract, like aging parents;
Soon now the war will shutter the grand hotels;
And we, when we come back, must come as parents.
There are no lanterns now strung between pines—
Only, like history, the stark bare northern pines.

And after a time the lakefront disappears
Into the stubborn verses of its exiles
Or a few gifted sketches of old piers.
It rains perhaps on the other side of the heart;
Then we remember, whether we would or no.
—Nostalgia comes with the smell of rain, you know.

from *Antaeus*

Hercules Musarum

◇ ◇ ◇

after the coin of Pomponius Musa

Be strong this way.

Your hat somebody's skin,
a lion fell,
its teeth grip your hairline,
its paws upon your paps.

Be Hercules be strong
be fifty years old like me
and under the grizzle and muscle and flab
find a secret woman
doing woman things with music . . .

call her the Muses.
Be for her.

No one else will ever listen so well
and you will never have to imagine so clearly
as you do now, to hear her,
to keep hearing her
so the phorminx in your fingers
keeps up its jive and the scroll
of continuous poetry unrolls
from her mouth in your mouth
like an old dog with a sloppy tongue,

infelicitous comparison
for your noble epyllion.
Old old old old . . .
be not afraid to repeat,
be not afraid to listen well

and chant what you hear
husky strong voice with a beat in it,

your thirteenth labor:
clearing your throat.

And when you are tired of music,
let your eyes fall open of themselves
and see the landscape she proposes;

inside from outside you can't distinguish,
one continuous ribbon of road
where you meet simultaneously
but separately everything that ever
happened to you. Here
is that fierce lion and that fiercer boarpig,
the nasty birds and Triton's coils.

See it clearly, see it gold,
see every twist of hair and every
glint on gilded shield,
see it clearly and it all
falls into the world around us
as the world.

Song, saying, seeing: these
are enough to reckon
your measure, Old One, Valiant One,
strongest listener.

from *Tyuonyi*

KEVIN KILLIAN

Pasolini

◇ ◇ ◇

First, after the spots in the Sun
the twenty-seven holes in the coronal
Then, the meeting in the hotel
with a man in a cape only more discreet   Visconti

First, look at that blackened scar
an elbow like a piece of macaroni
Then on the plate
I nearly came while I was looking   "No Hands"

first, both ways, crossing the
street to the traffic island
Then a big van painted multicolor
hippie style, a tiger across it   The 60s

First, why don't you shave
your filthy face is burnt with oil
Then you could maybe eat
a bit of fruit like maybe, my little guava   foreplay

First in the Mezzanine Palace
of the ancestors
Last on my list of like
required reading, get it?   Lovecraft

from *Shiny International*

AUGUST KLEINZAHLER

Soda Water with a Boyhood Friend

◇ ◇ ◇

He is in the canals behind your forehead
paddling,
        or in the high vaulted rooms
your speech
rays around itself, checking
the physics
of a dropped dime
resonating against what he has down
in the log of his remembering . . .

over a cigar and club soda. Ah,
the forests,
the good jungle, deluged with scene mutating
scene breeding scene,
fuckingchoking to death
a regular Mardi Gras on LSD
wired into your EEG
and beamed off satellite
to multitudes of kindled selves.

from *New American Writing*

Movement Along the Frieze

◇　◇　◇

Who are these people who have got their grammar and their diction
    levels
the way they want them. Who are their sweethearts
and who is their friend that they call up in McKeesport
and say something to. A plain tale. Please like their work.
Please like what men and women and children present the
line-breaks of. How did they get their act together
in the matter of sentence fragments, which are sacraments,
and of all those Nortony things, in their English-teacher costumes
or barn clothes and out partying in Bayonne, New Jersey, writing
    stuff down all the time.
Please anyway read what they brought out of the despair
of the boringness of expected word order and what got printed with
    margins
on four sides of it, in what somebody else, a graphics person,
figured out for a typeface; oh please like all these
and the cover of paper which is supposed to decompose
so that they will have something to write their elegiac and mutability
poems about, some of them even MID-party arguing in oral comma
    splice
that written comma splice is a form of parallel structure
and so not only justified but welcome! and others loudly disagreeing
totally. (And one of the noisiest avers that incremental repetition
is a form of parallel structure!) Some write syntax down goofy
and then go back and put profundity in
—which is fine—in an air of peace and freedom
as some of them have fasted or will fast or otherwise

sacrifice. A trace of movement along the frieze.
"For a symbolic hand," says this one or the other,
"lies on the pulse of protean co-Americans,
the very hand on the light table, the gong's mallet,
an instrument like my word: confusion of stillness
and motion, the *horror vacui,* and the ancient
nobility of fictive farce!" Perhaps, please,
among blot and stipple and among these nattering damned
didactic SAT and vocabulary words, which are boring
or stunning (in exigency of plot as metaphor) sometimes
to read, the poems are honored by your time and attention.

from *New American Writing*

What People Say About Paris

◇ ◇ ◇

They often begin by saying, "Paris! How I wish I were there!"
Someone said, "Paris is where good Americans go when
    they die."
"Pit pat, pit pit patter," say the raindrops
Falling on Paris in Apollinaire's poem "La Pluie."
"I was so happy in Paris," I said. "It was like
Loving somebody. The first three times I left there, I cried."
"I don't like Paris," say some. And others, "Paris is getting
    nice again."
"If you don't meet anyone but concierges and waiters,
How can you like any place?" Another says, "The French do
    not have friends,
They have relatives." A Frenchman says, "Le français n'est
    pas intelligent,
Il est rapide." "Paris is ruined," say certain, all the time.
"Paris was at its best in the nineteenth century."
"Paris was wonderful between the wars." "Old Paris is no
    more,"
Said Baudelaire. "The form of a city
Changes more quickly, alas! than a mortal's heart!"
"Paris! Like the dial of a clock!" cried one. And another,
"Give me the bottle of whiskey and I'll go with you to Paris!"
It is said: "Paris in the spring!"

One day the girls were clustered on the street corner
And the boys were moving toward them with their eyes.
The automobiles sped past and let this happen.

It is not like the primitive joys
Of Africa to be be-spattered by perfumes
And breast culture in the midst of a tramway crossing
Of gulfs, gulches, and wild cliffs of every imaginable costume.

"Come into the telephone kiosk with me,"
Said the French mother to the blue-shorts-clad boy.
"I am your son," he gallantly whispered,
"And I shall do as you say." Later the mother's breasts popped
    open
To her lover, on the avenue Marc Chalfont. The boy played
    with an owl.
Three years later he entered the Lycée Fromentin
From which we see him carrying a yellow notebook now
On his way home to the rue Descaligues, where his little
    family,
Still together, despite his mother's fooling
Around, has a second-floor apartment full of charm—
Its old but attractive furniture welcomes the boy
Who flings himself into an ancient armchair's arms.

No longer does one walk up the Iambic street
To fire the bathwater there, an elegant freak,
For the bathtub industry has conquered this city of dreams.

Lovers found ways to clown around elsewhere.
Earlier, the combination of obligatory openness
With old-fashionedness gave thrills of an erotic hide-and-seek
With comfortableness no longer to be found, even considered.

My Paris was not your Paris
And your Paris was not mine.
We both sat down on the quick white Valentine
Of the torsoed curb that makes December Alpine.

The sun shines. Paris must be earning a living.
I take myself out with my walk. Then my walk leaves me
And I realize that the sun is shining on me.

The cool men of Paris move back and forth
From woman to woman, table to table, word to word.
The warmer men are confused
But feel superior to the cool ones who feel
Superior to them. A wind blows
The shutters open, till there is a certain degree of shine.

"Ah, you are a poet!" said the waiter
At La Rotonde, "and I,
I have the name of a poet: Francis Jammes!"
"How did this come about?" I said
When he came back with his napkin
Like a white flag. "My father just
Gave it to me." "He liked Jammes's
Poetry?" "No, I don't
Think he'd read it. Neither have I.
It's true, I have a name that is quite well-known!"

In Paris I was never mute.
"I was once a cab driver in Beirut,"
Someone said to me. And, "I am a member of the Institute."

The social life, you say, is too limited in Paris.
Also, "Paris is a small town, unlike New York."
"You can no longer find any courtesy in Paris." "People have
    again become courteous in Paris."
"Only an American and a sentimental fool would write this
    way about Paris—
Places don't really mean anything any more." "Paris, it is
A beautiful woman!" "Paris, it is a giant's hip bone."
"Paris is the center of a maze
Whose entrance is in Rome." "I should never have told you
    about Paris.
Now you will come here and ruin it for me."

"I wish that I had grown up in Paris." "You know nothing of
   Paris."
"Henry James met Turgenev in Paris."
"The best thing in life is to be young and in Paris."
"I have never been so lonely as I've been in Paris."
"Dogs are allowed in restaurants in Paris." "Paris is ruined."
   "On Christmas Eve in Paris
Everyone stays up until dawn." "You can have chocolate in
   the morning instead of coffee." "I never want to leave."
"Paris is the largest Arab city in the world."

from *Poetry*

Mistral

◇　◇　◇

1.

There seems to be, about certain lives,
A vague, violent frame, an imperceptible
Halo of uncertainty, diffidence and taste
Worn like a private name that only God knows,
Echoing what it hides, that floats above a bottomless
Anxiety that underlies their aura of remote calm.
The intense half-dreams accumulate behind a smile;
The mind hesitates in its reflection, but remains alone.
Part of their story is an emptiness that isn't there,
But that holds the rest in a kind of desperate embrace
Until the rest is still, and the loneliness reverberates
With the breathing of an almost human kind of peace.
But the contentment is imaginary, and the tenderness,
Like the tree in God's mind, a figment of contemplation.

The feeling alters or the memory wanes, leaving the mind
Still waiting aimlessly, in the light trance of time,
While the incidents shine on a receding screen,
Or a remark hangs, or some impulse lingers unfulfilled
While love fades, until only a deep difference lasts.
Sometimes at night, when the past opens and the buried
Longings wrap themselves in colors, it almost starts
To seem as though another form of life were possible:
That although anger and love are real, the smaller,
Transitory emotions are real too, and more alive.
Day brings a sense of distance and the schematic moods
Of the depicted life—vacuity, release and friction,

But behind the friction and the pretense of indifference,
A conception of life as infinitely far away. And the sense
Is sharper, the imagination unrelenting in its isolation,
Yet sometimes, after a walk on a fine morning or a quiet
Meal in the little restaurant, absorbed, for a moment,
In the fleeting pleasures of the afternoon.

2.

Somewhere in the initial, lost experience of fiction
There is a phase of detachment, a dense, irrational
Feeling of enchantment mingled with a sense of loss
So abstract that it must have made the differences
Between memory and the imagination seem almost unreal.
Life wanders or the mind strays, but the story holds,
With the flat, incantatory tones embodying the desire
For consecrated moments and the need for repetition
In the same reflexive images, but becoming stranger,
Until they start to seem something like other people,
Or like figures in some stylized tableau set vaguely
On a coast in midsummer, with the sun shining madly
And the houses strung like pearls above an azure sea.

He was sitting on the terrace with a group of friends,
Lost in another of those vacant, sentimental reveries
About aging and the afternoon, or about how intricately
The summer day ends, or about clothes, or about light.
Along the beach a few waves moved, as the summer
    people
Watched the gulls descend in slow, exhilarating glides.
Now and then he made a desultory remark, just to amuse,
But his mind was elsewhere, quietly contemplating some
Provisional conception of himself, paradoxically young
But with some of the details rendered slightly indistinct
By too much passive sensation, and the bright, distracted
Conversation getting more private every year from an excess
Of gin and sun, yet the overall bearing marvelously alert,

Even in repose: the delicate, angular head, rich-old, with
Light, dry hair and eyes that lock and suddenly look away;
The thin, impeccable English shirting; the expensive skin.

He was forty-eight, and still waiting for somebody to adore
Without wanting, or without the ultimate possibility of
     loss.
His life felt as though it were always just about to start
Or end, or about to become relatively clear; but for now,
Temporary alliances would do, and the minor moods that
     last
All afternoon, waiting upon the mild exigencies of
     summer,
Rehearsing the fashionable despondencies, or trashing N.
He was all alone, with a range of sympathy unable to extend
Beyond the glass sphere of consciousness, where he lived
In an illusion of the complacency he'd always wanted, like
A dreamer clinging tightly to what he doesn't have
     anymore,
Or the mind instinctively reflecting what it can't become.
And then gradually it started to slip away, leaving him
Like someone in his own imagination, fabricating his past,
Breathing in the fragrance of depleted rage and each day
Looking forward helplessly, in perplexity or pain, until
He was beyond forgetting. But he kept it for a while, like
The love he'd held in his hands, then lost in wealth and
Memory abandoned it to tenderness, to the magnification
Of feeling, and to the solitary pretense of regret.

He continued to inhabit his imagination, but with a sharp
Sensation of the way time passes, while its illusion lasts.
He began to think of his life as an interminable
     preparation
Cast in the form of a reminiscence, with an extended part
In the present tense intended for the contemplation of
     those
Light boats, and with a phase of indifference followed by a
Sense of exhaustion and a perfunctory ending, for that was

How, eventually, his own renaissance was going to come:
Not in a flood of inspiration, but through an interval of
Change so long that it was going to feel like the
    meticulous
Development of one constant theme. And then one day
He realized he'd lost the past. There wasn't any
Inevitability anymore, and the imaginary differences
That used to seem so final didn't matter now—
There was just life, but part of his soul was dead
And the rest was waiting in the garden, where a little
Breeze rustled the paper lanterns. Maybe later a
Kind of character would emerge, but that would have
To be in the imagery of another life: the vague,
Abstract affairs, and the distracted way
Love swept the ruins; the play of conversation
And sunlight on a tessellated floor;
The buried stairs.

3.

            Deep inner dark
Where the violence gleams and the indifferent
Face that only God sees looks up from the water
With its relentless smile, while its features shatter
And float away and its lineaments start to disintegrate
Into shimmering, light and dark patches, which one day
Were going to come to seem like elements of happiness.
Sometimes the fragments can illuminate the enormity of
    the years
And how the soul is lost in them, as in a form of memory
In which there aren't any disillusionments or dreams,
But where it can be seen in its entirety, in an impersonal
    perspective
And without feeling, or lifted out of its isolated context
Like an inert thing and suspended there until the vertigo
    subsides
And the illusion that the years converge on it returns.

In dreams, or in these moments of distraction that derive
   from dreams,
Sometimes the waiting can begin to seem so real that the
   illusion fades
Into the security of home, as though everyone else had
   gone
While the night-light had continued burning, and the
   future
Had been transformed into an infinite field of possibility
   again.
Yet in that closed, capacious chamber where his real soul
Inhabited its shadowy mythology of light and recollection,
Delusive memories and self-fulfilling expectations glowed
   and disappeared
In the darkness where he waited patiently, held spellbound
By his mirror-image, and by the years collapsing inward in
   concentric waves.
For the past was over, and tomorrow had dwindled to a
   pin,
While the person in the water had gradually become as
   alien to him
As the sound of his own voice, as though the characteristic
   words
Were being spoken by a stranger, in a language he couldn't
   comprehend,
As he listened to the grandiose and convoluted explanation
Without any real sense of understanding, captivated by the
   air of intellect
And the inverted anger, glaring down at the deserted
   surface
In abject despondency, yet finally acquiescing in its flat,
Fastidious music, with its insistent undertone of sadness
And its persistent tendency towards abstraction, like a
   fallacious
Argument against the disenchantment that was going to
   come
Eventually, in the amorphous future, when the twin spells
Would loosen and their two trajectories would intersect.

It's milder now. Summer is ending with the human
    imagery
Strewn everywhere like fragmentary objects, exhausted by
    his dreams
And shattered by the sublimated intensity of his actual
    desires.
And it gets easier to see, yet the rest is still almost
    impossible to understand
Completely, as their faces vanish like despondent ghosts
Into the thin air of consciousness, while the secondary
    voices
Sleeplessly repeat the customary sanctifying consolations
In their private language, leaving, at the center of the
    imagination,
Just a blank expanse where people merely illustrate each
    other,
Featureless and flat. But then none of them were real.
It was a waste of feeling, though the aspiration mattered
For its vision of the separate sense of life it would have
    made
As tangible as the slow hallucination of a summer day;
For he was something more and less than a mirage, a
    hollow
Simulacrum of that hidden world of feeling and
    resentment
Where the mind creates its own peculiar history, and its
    way of looking
Back upon itself as through a stranger's eyes, as through a
    mirror.
And the result is free, like the animula that flourishes in
    solitude
Or in that cave of recollection where the colors coalesce
Behind the doppelganger's death mask, hovering out of
    reach somewhere beyond
The range of consciousness, as though the soul were just a
    story something told
Whose spell was memory and whose quiet theme the
    deepening sense of isolation

Memory brings, until the years begin to seem like stages
Life goes through while love deteriorates and disappears
Into a state of feeling, and then a phase of play and
    introjection,
Abnegation and exculpatory gestures, and finally into a
    subjective scream.
But he was an idea, and only an idea can dissolve this way,
Like God, into the mystery of someone else. And only in
The guise of a reflection can the soul's intense immediacy
    be apprehended,
Freed from its prison of personality and the contingencies
    of character
Into a condition beyond certainty, in which nothing
    changes
And it remains alone, in an oblique kind of happiness,
Bathed in the furious transparency that separates it from
Another person's dense, unimaginable interior reality.

4.

Time passes, as a cold wind sweeps the summer shapes
    away
At the release of autumn, while the intervals between the
    years
Become shorter, and the illusion of their real significance
Becomes more and more attenuated, and finally
    disappears.
I used to think that everyone's life was different, and that
    nobody could change
Except by dying, or by gradually withdrawing from the
    world
Into the mind of God, into the fantasy of being seen for
    what he was
Objectively, by someone else, in solitude. Day after day
The portrait becomes vaguer as the mind disintegrates,
Yet the essential core of secrecy remains, and the strange
    sensation

That this sense of life I thought that other people knew so
    well is mine alone.
The illusion is depth. The banality at the heart of things
In which the heart can rest and let its final feelings form
Lies on the surface, and the transitory moods that seemed
    to deepen into life
Vanish like wishes now, like words. What remains behind
Is a kind of feeling of contingency, a gradual waning of the
    present
Into a mere possibility, as though it were a dream of the
    extent of life
In which there wasn't any tangible experience of finitude,
    only a dull,
Unfocused anger as the words slide off the page and out of
    memory,
And the faces wash away like caricatures on a wall, and the
    sky fades.
I sometimes think of writing as a way of effacing people,
    of transforming them into ideas
By way of saving them, or of restoring them to that
    abstract state of innocence
From which the burden of the concrete personality
    descends.
Like sounds in sleep, unreal beyond the confines of their
    dream,
This force of life beyond intelligence maintains its surge,
But with a separate person cloistered in each moment like
    eternity,
Cut off from others by the wall of consciousness and from
    itself by
Time, the form of consciousness, as though to exist at all
Were to remain alone. And yet I'd wanted to remain still
And let the light of recollection flow around me like the
    gradual
Absolution of the world by darkness, on the verge of sleep.
The common sense of things intensifies, and then dissolves
    away,

Until a fear of something deep within myself, inert and
    old,
Is what I have to live in, and the tone of my own voice all
    I can hear.
What happened to the winds that used to blow from
    nowhere?
But it flows in one direction, and the imagery that used to
    seem transparent
Is part of its history now, like the dead leaves of fiction,
And the passages that glowed with inner life give back the
    blank,
Insensate stare that means their intimations of another
    form of life were meaningless.
I know the inside of one story, yet the incessant ache that
Saturates its pages speaks to no one, and its nuances of
Light and thought and feeling aren't reflections of the real
Person who exists and changes, but of the bare soul
    alone—
Because by starting from another person's life and going
    on from there
I'd thought, that way, I'd come to feel the difference more
    deeply;
And because I'd wanted this to be something other than a
    poem.
This is all there is. And the year has come around again,
The days are longer and the high, thin clouds that gather
    in the atmosphere
Like afterthoughts inside the nearly empty mind don't
    seem as strange now
As they did a little while ago, before my fear of finding no
    one had abated
And the waiting started that has come to seem like
    happiness,
A condition of mere being, of year to year inhabiting the
    same
Repetitive illusion until now I feel suspended in its single
    thought,
As though my world had finally dwindled down to this,
    and left me here.

And as the years go by these remnants of a future I once
    had
Are also going to fade and my indifference deepen; yet
    somehow the mind,
Even in abstraction, seems bound to go on issuing its faint,
Disruptive cries of disagreement that conceal it as it turns
    away,
Distracted by the sense of something real and unattainable
That I know now is going to characterize my life until I
    die.
It's not so bad though: no one remembers what the world
    was actually like
On those first evenings, and the poetry that comes and
    goes
Eradicates all trace of their implicit promises that God
    was listening
And that time was going to answer in agreement; and it
    doesn't matter
That instead of being happy I am merely older, for the
    same
Impatience with myself that brought this private dream to
    life
Will surely vanish with it, leaving me alone inside a
    stranger
World than I remember, without any inkling of its
    underlying
Emptiness, or of having lived here in a kind of wordless
    paradise
Where nothing changes, now that everything has changed.

from *The Paris Review*

Unachieved

◇ ◇ ◇

Compared to the transcendental realm, the world under the
  roofed-in-cave is somber
but the colors, signatures
five senses and the sixth, their purifier
                touch by imagination's feather
   sight & sound of liquid flight from those waters the spirit
skyrs

Beauty comes to it at the heart's desire
to transmute out of pleasure's pleasure a distillation of birds into
  visionary symbols
the processional of variable coloration of finches, choral lights,
  that and the shadow we brood

I, in the wild state, inner feelings soar
Transcendence the mental dance imagines, but for an instant, as
  dear Bryant returning to stone
                    The starry sky, Pluto's mirror
The way you could talk about your life, splinters off a
  carpenter's floor under a microscope, those perfect symmetries
  or better, visible shavings, but never the tool
Invisible something may strike through the black room of higher
  perfection
self-torture in the humanisphere a sure thing before a whole
  forest revolves to sign a bio-regional imperative

consensus of the Hopi Way Separatist communes of no more
  than three thousand souls
                              Dianas out of Gaea's caves
this window does not fade from view in the coming pre-industrial
  age
retrieved in a narrow shoal where a Gull Feather given in bliss
  turns the deranged corpse in ritual passes
healing prayers legitimize to exorcize the sick stain of being that
  death, die, at sight of the Androgynous Republic
Drums of magic, *salve,*
                              caught here
to return to the caesura, the interrupted fault line Frisco day
  which tunnels avian thought
Everytime I think I'll turn off the main vein, quotidian concerns
  take over initiating script (social realities relative to mediocrity)
  where you cut it, different than esoteric cant
but lingually deeper into it, like "cut it" regarding the sacred
  science

. . . this flow of thought is different for the surrealist than for the
  rationalist diehard
that is, I refuse to "come to my senses" since Ah'm in 'em
Emotion signs this pain you're at the terminal syndrome Fabulous
  tunnels turn inner to bring up The Transcendent World
  Anew (it's never what you thought it was)
What I'm getting at is, why don't you examine with great care
  your entire body of death?
                              And
reorient the auditor to a gnosis so mystical the tree bark from
  which it claws refuses to inscribe whiteness
One with the supreme ego
                              nothing more elegant on the avian
  plane
flicker mandibles arrange the dwelling
and from all the gifts of Gaea, head for their origin:

In my dream, the Goddess in her heavenly palace on the
   earth
a kind of Marienbad in lunar light
She in her silver gown slightly décolleté
has me watch the Stellar Mirror
while stars of the Pleiades run in a rhythm of Eight
and do an astral dance, *tout court*

(I tell you, very matter of factly, this Dream though many years
   old has forced itself to be told)

Thus begins it, Love, she and the avatar in the Bo-Tree Garden
and consider from where I'm situated here in the Far West

            green lightning at Thunder's coast
looking east to Pharaonic Egypt where the West began
              bonsai trees among the pines
a swan's luminous power in air of mist

         haunted redwood shadows
world immortal because AMOR wove a tissue clear to specular
   sight
Wings of this city
            an otherwise haunted hillscape
             ultimate YS
Frisco once also covered with ancient waves
a kind of lost Atlantis several kalpas ago
its seven hills imagine old traditions of jazz

          Harmony is that secret
between the machines coming through Death is that machine
the wild wee drop
         snow to the solar radiant a fumbled perfected
  Rebus of mental luminoids
            music married to meaning when

the orange
almost red–streaked crest
magnifies millet
            to mark off the duration:
Ornithos
      gold
      a parabola
                  The treasure perch is you and me, love
a tiny winged fiery tongue through the green window
                                          Forms are
      weddings
that spring trays of meaning between chirps
flutes garner ellipses of word
fork between eclipses of comet-lore across lagoons

            salt
from the Mediterranean Sea fixed here at Nova Albion
A boy painting earth colors above the valley town
my first poetry atop San Bruno Mountain was all power ek-stasis
as if all tracks had left the last railway station
the sensation of sudden union with another attraction
to decipher no matter what suffering there's no pain at the taste
      that tells an epic begins
brown & red over the mental rainbow
not to close this grandeur beyond words?
War mental war and no other These the weapons on the highest
      nest Golden V sang to Violent Ocean
It was forbidden to know what the melting glyphs said over the
      horizon
the ways down in the valley flowed away like darkness painting
      poetry to light
At this stage of the great game you can assassinate all the stand-ins
      with cosmic disdain *El Poder del Niño Jesus*
In the dreams of the Philippine "master" late of Frisco gone to
      Alaska
"Joke's on you" The Plague reminds The Fluke
Grey cant explosions through cells
prisons rent to specular essence

where it counts . . . is it laughter?
The old necromancer calls 'em up every day faster than thought
　Ibis eye of the Sacred Geomant
Gaea doing this dance down on the plain
coming of the inland sea where once there was none
I begin to steal Gaea
but Gaea is another circle of the rose Pantheism of the moment
where all rivers meet from the mountaintop

Caveat emptor!

Thunder for Gaea who's more than thunder
mysterious as in the beginning
Gaea the more I say you the seldom I leap through you
to my own ego
　　　　　upon the bread your birds beak

this look of red-crowned avifauna

the moon conjuncts Saturn
　　NOW
　　and
　　today

from *Sulfur*

Psyche's Dream

◇ ◇ ◇

If dreams could dream, beyond the canon of landscapes
Already saved from decorum, including mute
Illicit girls cowering under eaves
Where the books are stacked and which they
Pillage, hoping to find not events but response

If dreams could dream, free from the damp crypt
And from the bridge where she went
To watch the spill and the tree
Standing on its head, huge and rootless
(Of which the wasp is a cruel illustration

Although its sting is not), the decay
Now spread into the gardens, their beds
Tethered to weeds and to all other intrusions;
Then the perishing house, lost from view
So she must, and you, look out to see
Not it but an image of it, would be

Nowhere and would not resemble, but would languish
On the other side of place where the winged boy
Touches her ear far from anywhere
But gathered like evening around her waist
So that within each dream is another, remote
And mocking and a version of his mouth on her mouth.

from *Before Recollection*

DAVID LEHMAN

Operation Memory

◇ ◇ ◇

We were smoking some of this knockout weed when
Operation Memory was announced. To his separate bed
Each soldier went, counting backwards from a hundred
With a needle in his arm. And there I was, in the middle
Of a recession, in the middle of a strange city, between jobs
And apartments and wives. Nobody told me the gun was loaded.

We'd been drinking since early afternoon. I was loaded.
The doctor made me recite my name, rank, and serial number
    when
I woke up, sweating, in my civvies. All my friends had jobs
As professional liars, and most had partners who were good in bed.
What did I have? Just this feeling of always being in the middle
Of things, and the luck of looking younger than fifty.

At dawn I returned to draft headquarters. I was eighteen
And counting backwards. The interviewer asked one loaded
Question after another, such as why I often read the middle
Of novels, ignoring their beginnings and their ends. When
Had I decided to volunteer for intelligence work? "In bed
With a broad," I answered with locker-room bravado.
    The truth was, jobs

Were scarce, and working on Operation Memory was better than
    no job
At all. Unamused, the judge looked at his watch. It was 1970

By the time he spoke. Recommending clemency, he ordered
   me to go to bed
At noon and practice my disappearing act. Someone must have
   loaded
The harmless gun on the wall in Act I when
I was asleep. And there I was, without an alibi, in the middle

Of a journey down nameless, snow-covered streets, in the middle
Of a mystery—or a muddle. These were the jobs
That saved men's souls, or so I was told, but when
The orphans assembled for their annual reunion, ten
Years later, on the playing fields of Eton, each unloaded
A kit bag full of troubles, and smiled bravely, and went to bed.

Thanks to Operation Memory, each of us woke up in a
   different bed
Or coffin, with a different partner beside him, in the middle
Of a war that had never been declared. No one had time to load
His weapon or see to any of the dozen essential jobs
Preceding combat duty. And there I was, dodging bullets,
   merely one
In a million whose lucky number had come up. When

It happened, I was asleep in bed, and when I woke up,
It was over: I was 38, on the brink of middle age,
A succession of stupid jobs behind me, a loaded gun on my lap.

from *Shenandoah*

A Walk with Tom Jefferson

◇ ◇ ◇

Between the freeway
        and the gray conning towers
of the ballpark, miles
        of mostly vacant lots, once
a neighborhood of small
        two-storey wooden houses—
dwellings for immigrants
        from Ireland, Germany,
Poland, West Virginia,
        Mexico, Dodge Main.
A little world with only
        three seasons, or so we said—
one to get tired, one to get
        old, one to die.
No one puts in irises,
        and yet before March passes
the hard green blades push
        their way through
where firm lawns once were.
        The trunks of beech and locust
darken, the light new branches
        take the air. You can
smell the sticky sap rising
        in the maples, smell it

even over the wet stink
            of burned houses.
On this block seven houses
            are still here to be counted,
and if you count the shacks
            housing illegal chickens,
the pens for dogs, the tiny
            pig sty that is half cave . . .
and if you count them you can
            count the crows' nest
in the high beech tree
            at the corner, and you can
regard the beech tree itself
            bronzing in mid-morning light
as the mast of the great ship
            sailing us all back
into the 16th century
            or into the present age's
final discovery. (Better
            perhaps not to speak
of final anything, for
            this place was *finally* retired,
the books thrown away
            when after the town exploded
in '67 these houses
            were plundered for whatever
they had. Some burned
            to the ground, some
hung open, doorless, wide-eyed
            until hauled off
by the otherwise unemployable
            citizens of the county
to make room for the triumphant
            return of Mad Anthony Wayne,
Père Marquette, Cadillac,
            the badger, the wolverine,
the meadow lark, the benign
            long toothed bi-ped

with nothing on his mind.)
        During baseball season
the neighborhood's a thriving
        business for anyone
who can make change
        and a cardboard sign
that reads "Parking $3."
        He can stand on the curb
directing traffic and pretend
        the land is his.
On mid-August nights I come
        out here after ten
and watch the light rise
        from the great gray bowl
of the stadium, watch it catch
        a scrap of candy wrapper
in the wind, a soiled napkin
        or a peanut shell and turn
it into fire or the sound
        of fire as the whole world
holds its breath. In the last
        inning 50,000
pulling at the night
        air for one last scream.
They can drain the stars
        of light. No one
owns any of this.
        It's condemned,
but the money for the execution
        ran out three years ago.
Money is a dream, part
        of the lost past.
Joe Louis grew up a few miles
        east of here and attended
Bishop Elementary.
        No one recalls
a slender, dumbfounded
        boy afraid of his fifth grade

home room teacher. Tom Jefferson
    —"Same name as the other one"—
remembers Joe at seventeen
    all one sweltering summer
unloading bales of rags
    effortlessly from the trucks
that parked in the alley
    behind Wolfe Sanitary Wiping Cloth.
"Joe was beautiful,"
    is all he says, and we two
go dumb replaying Joe's
    glide across the ring
as he corners Schmeling
    and prepares to win
World War II. Like Joe
    Tom was up from Alabama,
like Joe he didn't talk
    much then, and even now
he passes a hand across
    his mouth when speaking
of the $5 day that lured
    his father from the cotton fields
and a one room shack the old folks
    talked about until
they went home first
    to visit and later to die.
Early afternoon behind
    his place, Tom's gathering up
the remnants of this year's
    garden—the burned
tomato plants and the hardy
    runners of summer squash
that dug into the chalky
    soil and won't let go.
He stuffs the dried remains
    into a supermarket shopping cart
to haul off to an empty block.
    The zinnias are left,

the asters in browns and dirty
        yellows, tough petalled
autumn blooms, even a few
        sticky green rose buds
climbing a telephone pole.
        Alabama is not so far back
it's lost in a swirl
        of memory. "I can see trees
behind the house. I do
        believe I still feel
winter mornings, all of us
        getting up from one bed
but for what I don't know."
        He tips his baseball cap
to the white ladies passing
        back the way we've come.
"We all come for $5
        a day and we got this!"
His arms spread wide to
        include block after block
of dumping grounds,
        old couches and settees
burst open, the white innards
        gone gray, cracked
and mangled chifforobes
        that long ago gave up
their secrets, yellow wooden
        ice boxes yawning
at the sky, their breath
        still fouled with years
of eating garlic sausage
        and refried beans,
the shattered rib cages
        of beds that couldn't hold
our ordinary serviceable dreams,
        blue mattresses stained
in earnest, the cracked
        toilet seats of genius,

whole market counters
        that once contained the red meats
we couldn't get enough of,
        burned out electric motors,
air conditioners
        we suffocated, and over all
an arctic wind from Canada
        which carries off
the final faint unseeable
        spasm of the desire
to be human and brings down
        the maple and elm leaves
of early October. If you follow
        their trail of burnished arrows
scuttling across curbs and cracked
        sidewalks they'll lead
you to the cellar hole of
        something or someone
called Dogman. "Making do,"
        says Tom Jefferson.
His neighbors swear
        someone runs on all fours
with his dog packs. They claim
        they can tell when
their own dogs feel the pull
        of the wild ones.
The women talk of lost
        house cats grown to the size
of cougars. They've heard them
        crashing through the dense
underbrush of the dumping
        grounds and found
huge paw tracks in the snow,
        the remains of drunks
and children caught out
        after dark, nothing but clean bones
revealed under ice when
        the spring rains come back.

"There ain't no kids
          around here," says Tom,
"But if there were, the bones
          be about the same size."
Tom has seen vapor rising
          through the missing floorboards,
clouds of it, and maybe
          animals and man
together producing a new
          variety of steam heat.
Even I have seen a brutish
          black mongrel Dane
in late afternoon, his coat
          snow flecked, rising
on his hind legs to over
          seven feet, hanging
over fences, peering in windows
          as though he yearned
to come back to what
          we were. Winter's in everything
we say—it's coming on—we see
          it in the mad swirl
of leaves and newspapers
          doing their dances.
We feel it as iron
          in the wind. We could escape,
each of us feels in
          his shuddering heart, take
the bridge south to Canada,
          but we don't. Instead we
hunker down, slump a little
          lower in our trousers
and go slow. One night soon
          I'll waken to a late quiet
and go out to see all this
          transformed, each junked car,
each dumping ground and battered
          hovel a hill

of mounded snow, every scrap
          of ugliness redeemed
under the light of a street lamp
          or the moon. From the dark tower
of the Renaissance Center Ford built
          to look down
on our degradation to the great
          Ford plant downriver blowing
its black breath in the face
          of creation, the one at Rouge
where he broke first our backs
          and then the rest, everything
silent, suspended in a new world
          like no other. For a moment
a few stars come out to share
          this witness. I won't believe it,
but Tom will. Tom Jefferson
          is a believer.
You can't plant winter vegetables
          if you aren't,
you can't plant anything, except
          maybe radishes.
You don't have to believe
          anything to grow
radishes. Early August he's got
          sweet corn
two feet above his head,
          he stretches
his arm to show where
          they grow to.
Tomatoes "remind you what tomatoes
          taste like."
He was planting before the Victory Gardens.
          His mother brought
the habit up from Alabama. She was
          growing greens
behind the house no matter how small
          her strip of land,

cosmos beside the back door,
        early things
like pansies along the fence.
        "Why she could go
into a bare field and find
        the purple flags,
wild, bring them home, half-
        dead dirty chicks
on the palm of her hand, and they'd
        grow. I could
never do that, I gave up trying
        fifty years ago."
It didn't take FDR
        and "The war effort"
to make a believer out of Tom.
        When he went off to war
his son Tom Jr. took over
        the garden and did
a job, the same son went off
        to Korea and didn't
come home, the son he seldom talks
        about, just as he
seldom talks about his three years
        in the Seabees
building airstrips so we could
        bomb Japan, doing
the war work he did at home
        for less pay.
A father puts down a spade, his son
        picks it up,
"That's Biblical," he says,
        "the son goes off,
the father takes up the spade
        again, that's Biblical."
He'd leave for work in the cold
        dark of December.
Later, out the high broken windows
        at Dodge Main

he'd see the snow falling
	silently and know
it was falling on the dark petals
	of the last rose,
know his wife was out
	back hunched
in her heavy gray sweater
	letting those first flakes
slowly settle into
	water on the warm
red flesh of the dime store
	plants Tom Jr.
put in on his own.
	Later he'd come home
in the early dark
	with snow on his hair,
tracking the dirty
	snow on her rug—
they say the dogs yellow
	it before it hits
the ground—and she would
	say nothing.
"That's Biblical," he says.
	"We couldn't even look
near each other
	for fear of how
one might make the other cry.
	That's Biblical,
knowing the other so well
	you know yourself,
being careful the way she was
	never to say nothing
or show the least sign."
	Tom picks a maple leaf
stiff backed and brown
	from the gutter,
holds it against the distant
	pale sky streaked

with contrails. Maybe even
           war is Biblical, maybe
even the poor white
           fighting the poor black
in this city for the same
           gray concrete housing,
the same gray jobs
           they both came
north for, maybe that's
           Biblical, the way
the Canaanites and the Philistines
           fought the Israelites,
and the Israelites killed
           the Amalekites
always for the same land.
           "God wanted Saul
to kill them down to the last lamb.
           He didn't,
and he went crazy. Back
           in the riots of '42
they did not kill us down
           to the last lamb.
They needed us making airfields
           the way they needed us
making Fords before the war,
           maybe that's why
they went crazy." There at the end
           of the street is his house,
his since he came home
           and could never leave.
The wisteria along the side
           has grown to the thickness
of his own wrist, the back yard
           is roses still, squash
coming on, onions in late
           bloom to be tricked
by the first cold, potatoes
           hidden underground,

they think, forever.
     "It's Biblical.
The way David plays for Saul so he
     can weep, and later
when his turn comes David
     weeps for Absalom.
It's Biblical, you cry,
     it's Biblical you don't,
either way. That's Biblical."
     What commandment
was broken to bring God's
     wrath down on these streets,
what did we wrong, going
     about our daily lives,
to work at all hours until
     the work dried up,
then sitting home until home
     became a curse
with the yellow light
     of afternoon falling
with all the weight of final
     judgment, I can't say.
It's Biblical, this season
     of color coming
to its end, the air swirling
     in tiny cyclones
of brown and red, the air
     swelling my lungs,
banging about my ears so that
     I almost think I hear
Tom say "Absalom" again, a name
     owed to autumn
and the autumn of his hopes.
     It's Biblical,
the little pyres pluming
     the afternoon gray and blue
on these corners, the calm
     of these childless streets,

a dog howling from a distant
        block, another answering,
the calls of the chained animals
        going back and forth
so plaintive and usual no one
        hears. The sparrows
fan out across the grassless yards
        busily seeking
whatever seeds the cold winds
        burst forth, and this
day is coming to its end
        with only the smallest
winter birds to keep
        the vigil. "We need
this season," Tom has said,
        but Tom believes
the roots need cold,
        the earth needs to turn
to ice and snow so a new fire
        can start up in the heart
of all that grows.
        He doesn't say that.
He doesn't say the heart
        of ice is fire waiting,
he doesn't say the new seed
        nestles in the old,
waiting, frozen, for the land
        to thaw and even these streets
of cracking blacktop long gone gray,
        the seven junked cars
the eye can note collapsed
        on slashed tires, their insides
drawn out for anything, he doesn't
        say all this is a lost land,
it's Biblical. He parks his chromed
        shopping cart under the porch,
brushes the dirt and leaves
        from his worn corduroy—

six feet of man, unbowed—
  and locks the knee-high gate
of his fence that could
  hold back no one,
smiles and says the one word,
  "Tomorrow," and goes in.
Later he'll put the porch light on,
  though no one's coming.
The crazy Indian colors
  are blooming as the sun
begins to go, deep maroons
  they tell us are the signs
of all the earth we've pumped
  into the sky.
The same rich browns the ground
  reveals after rain,
the veins of orange I've uncovered
  digging the yard
spring after spring. Never once
  have I found the least sign
that this was once the Indian's
  ground, perhaps a holy land,
not a single arrow head
  or shard, though I
have caught a sudden glint of
  what I didn't know
while turning over dirt I swore
  was never turned before
only to kneel to a bottle cap
  polished down
to anonymity or a wad
  of tinfoil
from an empty pack
  of Luckys, curled
to the shape of whatever
  vanished human hand
tossed it off. We were not
  idle hands. Still a kid

when I worked nights
        on the milling machines
at Cadillac transmission,
        another kid just up
from West Virginia asked me
        what was we making,
and I answered, I'm making
        2.25 an hour,
don't know what you're
        making, and he had
to correct me, gently, what was
        we making out of
this here metal, and I didn't know.
        Whatever it was we
made, we made of earth. Amazing earth,
        amazed perhaps
by all it's given us,
        as amazed as I
who stood one afternoon
        forty years ago
at a railroad crossing
        near Joy Road
as the Sherman tanks passed
        two to a flat-bed car,
on their way to a war,
        their long guns
frowning down identically, they
        passed some twenty minutes
or more while the tracks groaned,
        the trestle snapped
and sighed with so much stubborn
        weight of our going
Later, in the forge room
        at Chevy, now a man,
still making what I never knew,
        I stood in the silence
of the great presses slamming
        home, the roar of earth

striking the fired earth, the reds
      searing their glowing image
into the eye and brain,
      the oranges and roses
blooming in the mind long
      after, even in sleep.
What were we making out
      of this poor earth good
for so much giving and taking?
      (Beets the size of fists
by the thousands, cabbages
      as big as brains
year after year, whole cribs
      of peppers, great lakes
of sweet corn tumbling
      by the trailer load,
it gave and gave, and whatever
      we had it took.)
The place was called Chevy
      Gear & Axle—
it's gone now, gone to earth
      like so much here—
so perhaps we actually made
      gears and axles
for the millions of Chevies
      long dead or still to die.
It said that, "Chevrolet
      Gear & Axle"
right on the checks they paid
      us with, so I can
half-believe that's what we
      were making way back then.

from *The Paris Review*

Degree Four

◇ ◇ ◇

There though where they
were regardless,
elsewhere. Mat made of
tossed-off straw.

Tissuepaper
house worn atop the
head. Tissuepaper
boat, lit up
inside . . .
Vanishing thread,
bleached burlap
sack . . .
Took one step
forward, took
two steps . . .

Took to being taken
past the breaking
point, muttered
legless,
"Harsh light, be our
witness," wondering why
were they no match
for
drift.   Saw that this

was what history was, that
thing they'd heard of.
Ferried across Midnight
Creek on a caiman's
back . . .
Saw themselves made
to eat uncooked rice . . .

Kept in a room called
Búsinêngè Kámba, put
to work.   Saw this too
was what history was.
Desolate
seedpod,   mother-in-law's
tongue,   tongued rattle.
Footless romp, reflected
light on flooded
ground . . .

Rolled a
joint with gunpowder
inside, struck a match,
whispered, "This is
what history does."
Said, "Above sits
atop its Below, each
undoing the other
even though they
embrace."

Went up in smoke, lit
by feathers of light,
debris falling for
ages . . .

This as they thought,
　　what was known as
history, this the
　　　　　　loaded
gun carried under one's
　　　　　　　　coat . . .

　　"Wooed by fish under
　　shallow water . . ."
　　　　　　　　This
too their sense of
　　what history
　　　　　　was.
Fleeting glimpse of
　　what, reached for,
　　　　　　　faded,
　　fickle sense of what,
read with small sticks,
　　　　　　　caved
in

　　from *Conjunctions*

Funeral March for a Papagallo

◊ ◊ ◊

You look out yellowing leaves of
Reminding my father each time

Of families of institutions
Mental wards scratching

Leaving little thin things starkly
Visible again you would say

Windows barred horizontally
To escape fires in dank brick

You will be gone
Soon buildings

from *Aerial*

TOM MANDEL

Hungry and Waiting

◊ ◊ ◊

Everyone here has the same idea.
"My hand is of destroyed
gold. An asseverated
fountain breaks dirt
with the red flowers & herbs
that climb out of the
garden, so slowly that
they glide down the comfort
of the hill for years.
The enameled glow of time
slides through my life like dimes
through a nickel slot."
An amorous glow surrounds
them and attaches
a part of their
size to the single
temper of a radial cloud,
as latent colors pile up
in the impervious
backwater of love below.
All stars of morning singe you,
giving orders to endure.
During that meeting her war
was flashing, errant
targets, and wished flirtations.
Her war was a flashing errand.
I go crazy where we went

together. Put your Tenor
sax on the bed, clothes
on those magazines; be
funny, bounce. Take
a motel room in
the family home, man
just gallop away
with all of the salt
to make a mammoth gleam
that's shaking
in the seat of his dance
while confidential clouds stroke
my forehead.
Friendliness is not the same
as friendlessness.
A liquid and a glass
are near but not so near
as the elision of touch
is a gas. Stable
and distended, like
a marble in a mirror,
at an angle or otherwise
we float under a thin crust
of wisp, ourselves a great
unconscious borne on edge
in the unhinged plane
peeling away to radiated
paleness with painted points
crippled corners, and
ripples, a glory of wings
to perturb the motion of
purposeful bulk
into faint forward.
The edge is pulpy, but
borders of tomorrow hurtle
below cumuli of night,
until our destiny dips
under the cloudy crust

of a colorless valley
whose gray spherical interior
is clouded sky, and
movement crackles with resistance.
The sky blues to gray
through the thin menace of clustered
vapors.
Occasional clearings pierce the
monochromatic desert of grasp.
Secret clouds kindle a Valhalla
of our variance, and
only the faintest dye prevails,
dips of cloudy horizon.
A single point, and even that lapses,
is bliss to stretch
with none to touch.
Wagons pass in the gap
of authorization while
flip side attendants
loop the heavy rolls.
We round and we shot.
Meticulous with silver
the sky disappears
into a cut out enclosure.
But as I sought that haven
a streak of shangri-la sky
returned brighter than before
and on it a spot of hero's
blood was the horizon.
Credits roll up the
ravishing view. Clouds snake
under the doorman's
invading voice. A black
stripe trails downward
across the stormy quadrant
from the point of the
sun's last crust

to a touch of horizontal memory.
We turn back to black,
heart to smoke, cloud
to descending blues.

from *Sulfur*

"Histoire"

◊   ◊   ◊

Tina and Seth met in the midst of an overcrowded militarism.
"Like a drink?" he asked her. "They make great Alexanders over at
the Marxism-Leninism."
She agreed. They shared cocktails. They behaved cautiously, as in a
period of pre-fascism.
Afterwards he suggested dinner at a restaurant renowned for its
Maoism.
"O.K.," she said, but first she had to phone a friend about her ailing
Afghan, whose name was Racism.
Then she followed Seth across town past twilit alleys of sexism.

The waiter brought menus and announced the day's specials. He
treated them with condescending sexism,
So they had another drink. Tina started her meal with a dish of
militarism,
While Seth, who was hungrier, had a half portion of stuffed baked
racism.
Their main dishes were roast duck for Seth, and for Tina broiled
Marxism-Leninism.
Tina had pecan pie à la for dessert, Seth a compote of stewed
Maoism.
They lingered. Seth proposed a liqueur. They rejected sambuca and
agreed on fascism.

During the meal, Seth took the initiative. He inquired into Tina's
fascism,
About which she was reserved, not out of reticence but because
Seth's sexism
Had aroused in her a desire she felt she should hide—as though her
Maoism
Would willy-nilly betray her feelings for him. She was right. Even
her deliberate militarism
Couldn't keep Seth from realizing that his attraction was
reciprocated. His own Marxism-Leninism
Became manifest, in a compulsive way that piled the Ossa of
confusion on the Peleion of racism.

Next, what? Food finished, drinks drunk, bills paid—what racism
Might not swamp their yearning in an even greater confusion of
fascism?
But women are wiser than words. Tina rested her hand on his thigh
and, a-twinkle with Marxism-Leninism,
Asked him, "My place?" Clarity at once abounded under the
flood-lights of sexism,
They rose from the table, strode out, and he with the impetuousness
of young militarism
Hailed a cab to transport them to her lair, heaven-haven of Maoism.

In the taxi he soon kissed her. She let him unbutton her Maoism
And stroke her resilient skin, which was quivering with shudders of
racism.
When beneath her jeans he sensed the superior Lycra of her
militarism,
His longing almost strangled him. Her little tongue was as potent as
fascism
In its elusive certainty. He felt like then and there tearing off her
sexism
But he reminded himself: "Pleasure lies in patience, not in the greedy
violence of Marxism-Leninism."

Once home, she took over. She created a hungering aura of
Marxism-Leninism

As she slowly undressed him where he sat on her overstuffed
art-deco Maoism,

Making him keep still, so that she could indulge in caresses, in
sexism,

In the pursuit of knowing him. He groaned under the exactness of
her racism

—Fingertip sliding up his nape, nails incising his soles, teeth
nibbling his fascism.

At last she guided him to bed, and they lay down on a patchwork
of Old American militarism.

Biting his lips, he plunged his militarism into the popular context of
her Marxism-Leninism,

Easing one thumb into her fascism, with his free hand coddling the
tip of her Maoism,

Until, gasping with appreciative racism, both together sink into the
revealed glory of sexism.

from *Armenian Papers*

Holding the Thought of Love

◇ ◇ ◇

And to render harmless a bomb or the like
Of such a pouring in different directions of love
Love scattered not concentrated love talked about,
So let's not talk of love the diffuseness of which
Round our heads (that oriole's song) like on the platforms
Of the subways and at their stations is today defused
As if by the scattering of light rays in a photograph
Of the softened reflection of a truck in a bakery window

You know I both understand what we found out and I don't
Hiking alone is too complex like a slap in the face
Of any joyous appointment even for the making of money

Abandoned to too large a crack in the unideal sphere of lack of
        summer
When it's winter, of wisdom in the astronomical arts, we as A & B
Separated then conjoin to see the sights of Avenue C

from *Exquisite Corpse*

Farewell Performance

◊ ◊ ◊

For David Kalstone (1932–1986)

Art. It cures affliction. As lights go down and
Maestro lifts his wand, the unfailing sea change
starts within us. Limber alembics once more
make of the common

lot a pure, brief gold. At the end our bravos
call them back, sweat-soldered and leotarded,
back, again back—anything not to face the
fact that it's over.

You are gone. You'd caught like a cold their airy
lust for essence. Now, in the furnace parched to
ten or twelve light handfuls, a mortal gravel
sifted through fingers,

coarse yet grayly glimmering sublimate of
palace days, Strauss, Sidney, the lover's plaintive
Can't we just be friends? which your breakfast phone call
clothed in amusement,

this is what we paddled a neighbor's dinghy
out to scatter—Peter who grasped the buoy,
I who held the box underwater, freeing
all it contained. Past

sunny, fluent soundings that gruel of selfhood
taking manlike shape for one last jeté on
ghostly—wait, ah!—point into darkness vanished.
High up, a gull's wings

clapped. The house lights (always supposing, caro,
Earth remains your house) at their brightest set the
scene for good: true colors, the sun-warm hand to
cover my wet one. . . .

Back they come. How you would have loved it. We in
turn have risen. Pity and terror done with,
programs furled, lips parted, we jostle forward
eager to hail them,

more, to join the troupe—will a friend enroll us
one fine day? Strange, though. For up close their magic
self-destructs. Pale, dripping, with downcast eyes they've
seen where it led you.

from *Grand Street*

Public Television

◇ ◇ ◇

I'm always scared.   Aren't
you.   In the kitchen
everything is humming,
my mother comments
that what I'm reading
looks heavy.   I say
it isn't   it's
about television
and go on
to explain
structuralism &
Robert Young
& mention
Zeborah in
passing as
where I
got this
book—
and that's
all my
mother
heard, I
know it.

I don't
know
why you're

not calling
me this
morning.

Is it because
I only wrote
you one love
poem last
August or
is it that
you're ashamed of
me I
fume up the
small winding
hills of Man-
chester, Mass.

There but
for the
grace of
god go
I behind
a woman
my age
dragging
her two
children.

I hurry
home to
remember
which postcard
I forgot
to send.
Can I be
breezy in
a letter?

My mother's
gonna sit
by the
stove.   It's
cold in
the kitchen
in New
England.

The sportscasters
are funny
here & the
people eat
a lot and
aren't so
friendly but
they say
hello.

If you
haven't
called me
that does
mean some-
thing.   That
I should
mind my
own business
the new
way to
be.   There
is of course
a mass media,
the thing
that everyone
sees that
everyone knows
what does

everyone
know, do
they care?
Does it look
okay. Then
there's the
little private
world of
feelings, let's
call that
access.

I don't care
how it
looks, or
if we're
watched by
how many
billion viewers,
see, I am concerned
with having
the important
spot in
your heart
and a channel
to mine
I want
this beam
to be
long and
strong
and true.
Is it?

from *Shiny International*

ROUTE E

◇ ◇ ◇

Em,
Auntie
an extremely small person who is otherwise normally propor-
tioned. Any of the various gnatlike flies of the family Chironom-
idae, found worldwide; or any small person. Often a term of
endearment for a woman with some other name. Lucy and Ethel
at the nude beach. "My God, you've been writing down everything
I've said," she said, then took my hand and clasped it to her bare
breast, making it the more difficult. This was at the ninth annual
Skeletal Symposium in Sun Valley, Idaho. The first bus had no
poetry so I waited for the next, a kneeling bus with a Niedecker.
After several days of sun and temperatures in the seventies, winter
is found lying on our doorstep with a befuddled look. There's
another sentence I'd nearly forgotten. Why so many American poets
write like Wittgenstein, or Gertrude. At the center of the town
square they had constructed a small circle in the shape of the letter,
"E." The waters of the Cheat River, swollen by storm, swept away
entire passages of ROUTE U. All the information pylons on cam-
pus had been cloaked in khaki the week of my father's return from
Egypt. His slides were full of ellipses. Everyone in the photograph
drank 7UP, just as they had in Ecuador. Thad increased the volume
at this point so that I couldn't hear myself up the ante. It produced
an interesting effect, much like humming into a cement mixer.
How might I gesture to explain to some other what I mean when
I write the word, "here"? In the next room Anika was balancing
her books by lizard light. "Tut, tut, Em! don't talk so gloomily.
Do you know of any one, now, who has been hired to put me to

death?" said he smiling. No one was more elated by this announcement than our friend Kinch, who had, in fact, grown quite ashy in his complexion from confinement and grief, and was now thrown by this intelligence into the highest possible spirits. "Let me take your coat; and, Eph, see you to that trunk," said Mr. Gairie. "I'm going north, because I wish to emancipate and educate my children—you know I can't do it here." "Oh, this will explain," archly rejoined Esther, as she held up to view one of the tiny lace trimmed frocks that she was making in anticipation of the event that has been previously hinted. She could not restrain the tears as she dressed little Em, whose eyes were large with astonishment at being sent home from school at so early an hour.

from *Aerial*

Light As Air

◇ ◇ ◇

1

It's calm today. I sit outside, or inside by the window, and look out, and for a moment I realize my left hand is holding up my head. I see the light on everything, trees, hills, and clouds, and I do not see the trees, hills, and clouds. I see the light, and it plays over my mind that it is any day, not today, just day.

2

The wind is making the trees swoosh and the volume goes up and down. I have been sitting here for some time, at first looking out at the grass and trees and sky, and then, turning more and more into my mind and its noticing things, gradually looking at nothing of what was before my eyes. A great cutting slash arced across the last turn of the mental pathway I had wandered down and up, and was approaching me from the left. I cocked my head to that left. Slash, slash in the woods. My legs chilled. I will wait until I hear it once more, then I will get up and go inside.

Silence.

3

In times of trouble and despondency I turn to sportswear. I have just added to my wardrobe three pairs of pastel-colored shorts and four light-gray T-shirts and a yellow cotton pullover so elegant and offhand it must have been designed in France. I put on my new clothes, lace up my new white shoes, and see people. They say, "You look nice. Are those shorts new?"

"Yes, they are," I answer.

Then I go back home and sit on the porch under the sky in my new shorts.

4

I look at you sometimes when you're not aware of it. I look at you in those moments the way a stranger might so I can see you better than I usually do. And in fact you do always look fresh and new and similar to the person I think of as you. I love the way you look. And I feel happy just to be here looking at you, the way the dog sits at the feet of us, his great gods. I sit at the feet of the thing that is you. I look at your feet.

5

I take off my clothes and am in the air, me flowing through it and it flowing around me. I look to the right. The first cottages of the little village, the first houses of the town, the first buildings of the city: bones, flesh, and clothing. Air around it all. Air I cannot breathe, because I am also a structure I am moving past, a tomb, a monument, a big nothing.

6

He is a man of many vectors, that assemble and reassemble, the way music comes first from the air, then from a piece of wood grown in air. Then the air is in a museum in a country you are not permitted to enter at this time because your vectors are not in order. You must go home and reassemble your rods and cones: night is falling, the soft gray mist of his breath.

7

I dreamed I had become a tall hamburger piloting a plane going down in a remote jungle waving up at me with inexpensive green cardboard natives ecstatic at the arrival, at last, of their messiah. A radiant hamburger bun top opened above me as I floated softly into their gyrating angular green midst.

8

I come to a mental clearing where I can speak only from the heart. Free of the baggage of who I happen to be, and of all the porters who must carry the baggage, and the exorbitant taxi ride into a fuller version of the same small personality, I take, for what seems to be the first time in a long time, a breath that goes deeper than the bottom of the lungs, and in the pause that comes at the end of that breath there appears a little mirror, light fog on it clearing quickly.

9

The palm of my hand is in Sunday, groggy, sabbatical. The rest of me is in Wednesday, up there and to the left, in the sky. I see you need a light, though you have nothing to smoke. You left your smoking utensils in Thursday. Let me recall my hand and fetch them for you. There, now you are creating puffs. But they do not dissipate. They form shadow copies of my hand that is moving toward your face.

10

It dawns on me that I'm repeating myself. Another day and there I am, calm outside in the air with my hand returning along its vectors. In this mental clearing the photons are jumping all around the savages. Suddenly the witch doctor brings his face to mine and shouts, "Mgwabi! Mgwabi!" pointing to my photons. I reach up and take the light from his face and fold it with the fingers on my hands and it dawns on me that I'm repeating myself.

11

At the end of the light I raise my voice from down there to up here and you are not here. I could shout until the words change colors and it would make no difference. Your vectors are heading out away from the voice of my hand and toward what it is pointing to, that bright cloud over there, the one with the burning edges, handsome and lighter than air at last.

12

A cold streak runs through the sky now the color of wet cement that forms the body of the man whose brain is at a height of more miles than can be found on earth. This emotional absolute zero is like a spine conducting thick fog and thin rain through him, and when the sun's vectors approach his surface they turn and move parallel to it. Who is this big cement man? And how do I know whether or not he is the same who came this morning and threw on the power that sent the electricity branching through my heart?

13

It's dark today. I sit inside, my right hand touching my head. I look at the floor, the fabrics, the smoke from my mouth. It's as if there isn't any light, as if part of things being here is what light they have inseparable from themselves, not visible. The table doesn't stand for anything, although it remembers the tree. The table isn't immortal, though it hums a tune of going on forever. The table is in Friday, with me, both of us here in this dark, miserable day, and I have the feeling I'm smiling, though I'm not.

from *Boulevard*

From C

◊   ◊   ◊

Paper universe of primes
Flooded land flooded hand

House: herself in the mirror photographing herself

lies over then under

reticular figures

both speaking /

not speaking

There mute flooded paper curiously

"dust and moths"

house and loss

images I carry
down into this

"Now you cannot speak
and now . . ."

Unutterable

pages

of counterlight

in the fluid window

a dog sings songs

asking nothing

we cannot speak

stages

of what was not

the speaking says

in day's word for night

"mute as stalks"

("moths")

are figured there

from *O.blēk*

Politics

◇ ◇ ◇

Once there was a straight line which told how it got bent.
Someone died and the town was named:
Pittsburg, Piedmont, Emeryville.
The tree was planted and then cut down,
its leaves scattered by the magic hand of chance.
Now drugstores and hospitals
go through their days, with a profit to show at year's end.
A twelve thousand ton building at dusk adopts a certain realistic
    tone
that metaphors, archaisms, and plain old schizophrenia just can't
    budge.

Chance is a modern idea.
A page out of the book of dreams
can't just be any page, it has to be the very page
where your mother first noticed your father.
They lived in the middle ages, when the sword was still stuck
    fast in the stone and there was no distinction between God
    and wealth.
There was no time to be subtle: in the ambulance
the Queen of Hearts noticed the Page of Hearts
thus making him the King of Hearts.
But *you*, you nameless blush,
aren't even conceived yet and so aren't supposed to be there
reading, imagining all the names might mean.

There are examples of people overcoming chance,
achieving political embodiment, the posters suddenly materializing,
   ascending to the heaven of free air time,
the pure paranoia of unendable meaning, thus gaining
a status quite unlike the local hardware store,
   which might, in a few months, become a jogging store.

Suddenly I heard the car across the street call my name
and so I knew that this was my cue:
as I was saying, once there was a road
that never curved except to provide a bit of pleasure,
but here we are already at the hospital.

                    from *O.blēk*

The Hearts

◇ ◇ ◇

The legendary muscle that wants and grieves,
The organ of attachment, the pump of thrills
And troubles, clinging in stubborn colonies

Like pulpy shore-life battened on a jetty.
Slashed by the little deaths of sleep and pleasure,
They swell in the nurturing spasms of the waves,

Sucking to cling; and even in death itself—
Baked, frozen—they shrink to grip the granite harder.
"Rid yourself of attachments and aversions"—

But in her father's orchard, already, he says
He'd like to be her bird, and she says: Sweet, yes,
Yet I should kill thee with much cherishing,

Showing that she knows already—as Art Pepper,
That first time he takes heroin, already knows
That he will go to prison, and knows he'll suffer

And says, he needs to have it or die; and the one
Who makes the General lose the world for love
Lets him say, *would I had never seen her,* but Oh!

Says Enobarbus, Then you would have missed
A wonderful piece of work, which left unseen
Would bring less glory to your travels. Among

The creatures in the rock-torn surf, a wave
Of agitation, a gasp. A scholar quips,
Shakespeare was almost certainly homosexual,

Bisexual, or heterosexual, the sonnets
Provide no evidence on the matter. He writes
Romeo an extravagant speech on tears,

In the Italian manner, his teardrops cover
His chamber window, says the boy, he calls them crystals,
Inanely, and sings them to Juliet with his heart:

The almost certainly invented heart
Which Buddha denounces, in its endless changes
Forever jumping and moving, like an ape.

Over the poor beast's head the crystal fountain
Crashes illusions, the cold salt spume of pain
And meaningless distinction, as Buddha says,

But here in the crystal shower mouths are open
To sing, it is Lee Andrews and The Hearts
In 1957, singing *I sit in my room*

Looking out at the rain, My teardrops are
Like crystals, they cover my windowpane, the turns
Of these illusions we make become their glory:

To Buddha every distinct thing is illusion
And becoming is destruction, but still we sing
In the shower. I do. In the beginning God drenched

The Emptiness with images: the potter
Crosslegged at his wheel in Benares market
Making mud cups, another cup each second

Tapering up between his fingers, one more
To sell the tea-seller at a penny a dozen,
And tea a penny a cup. The customers smash

The empties, and waves of traffic grind the shards
To mud for new cups, in turn; and I keep one here
Next to me: holding it a while from out of the cloud

Of dust that rises from the shattered pieces,
The risen dust alive with fire, then settled
And soaked and whirling again on the wheel that turns

And looks on the world as on another cloud,
On everything the heart can grasp and throw away
As a passing cloud, with even Enlightenment

Itself another image, another cloud
To break and churn a salt foam over the heart
Like an anemone that sucks at clouds and makes

Itself with clouds and sings in clouds and covers
Its windowpane with clouds that blur and melt,
Until one clings and holds—as once in the Temple

In the time before the Temple was destroyed
A young priest saw the seraphim of the Lord:
Each had six wings, with two they covered their faces,

With two they covered their legs and feet, with two
They darted and hovered like dragonflies or perched
Like griffins in the shadows near the ceiling—

These are the visions, too barbarous for heaven
And too preposterous for belief on earth,
God sends to taunt his prophet with the truth

155

No one can see, that leads to who knows where.
A seraph took a live coal from the altar
And seared the prophet's lips, and so he spoke.

As the record ends, a coda in retard:
The Hearts in a shifting velvety *ah,* and *ah*
Prolonged again, and again as Lee Andrews

Reaches *ah* high for *I have to gain Faith, Hope*
And Charity, God only knows the girl
Who will love me—Oh! if we only could

Start over again! Then The Hearts chant the chords
Again a final time, *ah* and the record turns
Through all the music, and on into silence again.

from *The New Republic*

DONALD REVELL

St. Lucy's Day

◇ ◇ ◇

All I can put my hands on, even
my face in the dark window over the sink
staring out to the fading yard and inside
to the brightening kitchen behind my face,
staggers helpless a little sometimes
and then is propped up. What's important
is to try to notice each thing and then
know what stops it falling too far to save.
A child could worry about where the yard goes
at nightfall. And I'm here worrying
about the kitchen glaring behind me,
wanting me to fall into the deep end
of the part of the night after supper.
But unlike a child and unlike
mute things as easy to pity as to fear,
I know something and have a choice to make.
If I fall, I can choose what stops me.

History is laughing all the time,
shaking the little bridges between itself
and islands of freedom, the remote tribes there
talking themselves into a frenzy, forgetting
the one history lesson that matters.
The present is easy. It hangs there
like a rough pendant in the shape of a house.
You press a door. Everything inside is too small
to hurt you, easy to walk around

in ideal floor plans—tract house, cloister,
brownstone. Even easier to stand
at the sink and to consider your options.
As the yard fades, is it too late for me
to stagger through the window towards the dark house
at the fenceline, which is to say the past,
those uneasy rooms? Or better to fall
backwards into the deep end of the night ahead?

Easy to consider. Like collecting
water in a stone basin at the end
of a garden, letting time discover
its own economy, conduct its own
half measures of rescue invisibly
as everyone else does. But thought is the bad
economy of the helpless who keep thinking.
It melts like thin ice in a stone basin
disappearing from all directions into
its helpless center, the here and now
it cannot enlarge and cannot abandon.
There is no saving myself anywhere
but in the past or future, no rescue
but falling backwards or forwards, into the yard
or into the mixed company of tonight's guests.
Whatever stops me falling is my real life.
I take everything there seriously.

The dark house at the fenceline never shrinks.
Even as the days shorten into the skittish
rites of St. Lucy's Day, it gets bigger,
opening its crazy floor plan wider
for more things, for people I'd given up
hoping to see together. Impossible
to walk around inside there. And sweet, never
to be hurt by strangers in so much darkness.
The deep end of the night ahead is full
of strangers ready to talk into
the small hours, rehearsing what may never happen

in new words, brighter associations
of shadow and real flesh and the blue patterns
of a woman's tongue I could touch with my tongue.
Impossible to be a ghost there. And sweet,
never to hurt anyone twice in one lifetime.
So my lifetime gutters between two real lives.

If he is honest, anyone can tell you
the same thing—at any moment, on any
of the little bridges of crisis
shaken by history's laughter, anyone
knows enough to make the choice he must make
between trying to live in the past
or the future. And nothing more than trying
because the choice comes again and again
onto the thin ice we never completely
abandon. That's how important the unreal
easy life of the present remains in spite
of the dangers. If I fall, tonight I fall
but one way. The shadow and flesh and tongue
of a woman in the next room are not
for my life. The night ahead is too fast.
Home, which I shall never reach, stands at the fenceline,
dark, slow, and filling with days that will not get longer.

from *Poetry*

From Act I, Scene II of
Guards of the Heart

◊ ◊ ◊

Scene II

Directions: Mid-morning—just after the shopkeepers have
opened and the children are at school—A small
village, Sesmosa meets an old woman.

Sesmosa: (Thinking to herself as she sees the old woman in
the distance)
The years, bring little pain, yet they add.
Everything builds, somewhere, and takes a toll—
not at crossings or borders or bridges, but
rather, the outside coming in and staying—
too close to the beat, but by the river, pumping
echoes to shore washing upon the ears, ringing—
what the mind reflects through eyes before water—
at a time yet called and stalled, somewhere
in the actions yet to take place
yet remembered, somehow.
Though, not yet—
and was already.
As though time stopped, I look
there me, after befores.
And now.
How? I circle or turn or watch or am
involved.

She, there, yes, I remember, not
but feel or rehearse.
All too often, again, yes
there goes I
through time past, colliding forward
never moving
but yet at a place, to watch
and call to companions, to look
and fill spaces—
not with bodies or lies or even plans,
but with the simplest of smiles—
arching a plain back to what connects
before we moved in, before we moved
before we.
And she knows, not on the edge—
but where it gathers.

Directions: Sesmosa approaches nearer to old woman.
She finds her speaking to herself.

Sesmosa: Yes, you must hear or feel too.
What I think, speaks birds to the night.
When alone washes air between world and weeds
yet springing in cracks, placed in planes—
not in flight, but near borders of thought,
and what is fought, in attempts
to feel a touch, placed before minds
just out of reach, too simple to teach.

Directions: Sesmosa stops within hearing
distance of the old woman
and listens.

Old Woman: As on white cracks hanging by shadow—
nearly touching a space, hovering between moon
and light, as easy defined by weight and blue,
as to you nears by what can't be placed, but is.
Somehow too slow to come to rooms to lie to stop.

Turns yet not rehearsed, or even required, but are—
taken so lightly and reflected in teeth.
Where eyes glance at what's not met
and can't be replaced for never being.
And I say yes, bounced by walls and straw.
And we pull at each other in air, and hold—
revolvings as place as we make.
And I step back, and you forward, and repeat
hello to a place, once slipped in an instant,
shared back to an instant before, and realign—
the thought now gone to feeling—waiting words
to place lines between distance—
and touch, somehow known, somehow shared.

Directions: Old Woman doesn't acknowledge the
presence of Sesmosa. She seems distracted
and starts to walk away (After speech her
words grow faint and inaudible to audience &
Sesmosa).
Sesmosa stops her physically and
speaks.

Sesmosa: So how does one—
encounter one, who encounters so.
Much remains, though much is stalled—
bogged in mist by what is missed.
And yet held in mind before what is timed.
And I wait knowing, too full to fill
the find of what we lost.
So I look to no other.
And choice appears by chance, perhaps—
or roll, or die, or desire derived not
by what I make, but what I lack.

Old Woman: So you had to reach to touch, what (pause).
My eyes reflect years to your teeth and still
you pull not by rhythms, not by the moon, not by
        beams—
but by what seems out of place, wandering in blue.
Now falling to cracks that you make, that you lack.

Sesmosa: So how does one, share (pause).
What we called in air, isn't there—
a white to fill, what is missed by blue,
added to the weight that can't be replaced—
moving forward to an instant before, or to words.

from *Aerial*

Jumping-jack flash

◇ ◇ ◇

a young woman with
the pack on her back—grabbing the
hat off an old man's head seated
several rows—to one side—in the movie
theatre—from him being that—on
her part

       so—not being—the young
       woman having been restrained—though from
       grabbing the old man's hat off—from him
       being old—and saying this
       —wrestling—in the movie theatre
       with a man from the audience

the—reactionary
event—though in a
conservative setting—as
it being reactive—which may be
for something—still—occurring

to have—my—seen the
real event—of the corpses floating
in the river—for burial—before—though
which is—pictured—in the movie—with
the woman's having grabbed the hat from the old man
in the audience—destroying him—may be

bums or unattached—traveling—on
the street—they happened to have clustered—but
hostile—not toward me, who was walking and
bled in a gush—so that it was more
than should be

the young woman—hassling
the old man, who'd been
seated quietly—her—screaming
in—the movie theatre—saying
he was old—hurting him

their being hostile—who're riff-raff—or
traveling—become—but who're congregated on
the street—by a market—not from
that coming about—may be—or
me—up to that

or from—their being
that—not being—or from the men in
the bar—facing seated in a rim—whether—they've
become—riff-raff—as distinguished from other
people—or has nothing to do with that

the bleeding in a gush—which I did, walking
—where they are not involved—
in the setting—and not as an emotional
implication—for me—but
of that physically—and therefore—
not as their condition—who're bums

as sentimentality—being destroying
him—the old man—though the
substantive event
of that—may be—but in him
being that

—to—come close to—an
ass—a destroying person—now—not
a bum—or as that—but—
taken in by it—and so
reversed as some other person

to do it—as a common
thing—inebriated
and happy as a reason—and
so no longer
seen—in terms—of—something

    conformity—in the circumstance
    of being whatever one is—required to
    of the setting everyone's in—as a silly thing
    doing—and only that—as
    the event

the woman—having hassled
the old man—for that reason—
as involuntary on—later—
her part—and so unattached—
or seeming as that

the woman—constraining the
action—of someone—or oneself—among
her friends—as humiliating—to
the other—though not regarded
as that by those—and from that

    so there's only that
    setting—of her friends—and oriented by
    such a thing—as inebriated—not from it
    —oneself—not humiliated—or those others, who're
    part of that scene

stupid childish—behavior—leading
to—the corpse—which then had been floating on
the river—for burial—not from our
culture—and in the conjunction of the adult person being
or acting—as—a child

which don't—act—that way
any more—as the adult person
or what one conceptualized that as—so
the stupid childish—behavior—of the
grown person—as the action

      that would then be—the
      derivative thing—of oneself—
      but as an adult which is
      the reverse—in the world—
      in that behavior

not dependent—on
oneself—or
even responsible to it—in
society—which isn't
that—from it

      the men working—together—the boss
      with another man—so the derivative
      thing—as exhausting oneself though up to
      returning to the construction job the next day—and
      not being able to talk

forcing oneself—in terms of jobs—to
endure a kind—of life that one can't
stand—and just to have that job
or a series—though which
is a necessity—as not a derivative
thing

the men in a new bar—later—and wearing the
new wave clothes—and the delicately
tuned inner workings—muscular—
as not being like—them—or
riff-raff—of some—modest—means

the construction job—as forcing—though
out—of necessity—not humiliating
or as that—without the primary response
of that—up to going the next day, and as what oneself can't
stand

from *Conjunctions*

Let's All Hear It
for Mildred Bailey!

◊   ◊   ◊

The men's can at Café Society Uptown
was need I say it? Upstairs
and as I headed for the stairs I
stumbled slightly
not about to fall
and Mildred Bailey
swept by in a nifty outfit:
off-brown velvet
cut in a simple suit-effect
studded with brass nail heads
(her hair dressed with stark simplicity)
"Take it easy, Sonny," she
advised me and passed on to the supper-club
(surely no supper was
served at Café you-know-which?)
A star spoke to me
in person! No one
less than Mildred Bailey!

Downstairs I nursed one drink
(cheap is cheap)
and Mildred Bailey got it on
and the boys all stood and shouted
"Mama Won't You Scrap Your Fat?"
a lively number

during the brown-out
in war-haunted, death-smeared
NY

   Then things got better, greater:
Mildred Bailey sang immortal hits
indelibly
permanently
marked by that voice
with built-in laughter
perfect attack: always
on the note
not behind or above it
and the extra something nice
that was that voice
a quality, a sound she had
on a disc, a waxing
you know it: Mildred Bailey

   The night progressed:
a second drunk—oops—drink
(over there, boys, in what seemed
like silence box-cars rolled on
loaded with Jews, gypsies, nameless
forever others: The Final Solution
a dream of
Adolf Hitler:
Satan incarnate)
Mildred Bailey winds up the show
with a bouncy
number: when she gets back
to Brooklyn
from cheapo cruise ship
visitation:
Havana, Cuba
(then the door stood wide
to assorted thrills)
the next one in her life

ain't gonna be no loser, a clerk
oh no
"You can bet that he'll be Latin"

And Mildred Bailey, not
quite alone
in her upstate farmhouse
the rain is falling
she listens to another voice
somehow sadly
it is singing a song:
music
in a world gone wrong

from *Poetry*

Empathy for David Winfield

◇ ◇ ◇

Now I feel good when Dave Winfield
throws his bat and it goes spinning
toward the pitcher and looks
intentional to some amateurish to others
but certainly dangerous and loosened
"reckless passionate perhaps innocent"
This was my style
the style of the thrown bat
the style of Ryne Duren
blinded with drink as he later confessed
deranged in all the senses
as he threw balls out of the stadium
behind the batter's head
the impossible pitcher
with an underhand of symbolic force
a pitcher who could only hope
to see the batter
and Reader
I throw my bat at you

from *Diamonds Are Forever:*
Artists and Writers on Baseball

St. Thomas Aquinas

◇   ◇   ◇

I left parts of myself everywhere
The way absentminded people leave
Gloves and umbrellas
Whose colors are somber and have the air of endless misfortune.

I was on a park bench asleep.
It was like the Art of Ancient Egypt.
I didn't want to wake myself.
I took the evening train with my heart's heaviness for luggage.

"We give death to a child when we give it a doll,"
Said the woman who had read Djuna Barnes.
We whispered all night. She had been to Africa.
She had many stories to tell about the jungle.

I was already in New York City looking for work.
It was raining as in the old black and white movies.
I stood in many doorways in that city.
Once I asked a well-dressed man for the time.
He gave me a frightened look and walked out into the rain.

Since "man naturally desires happiness"
According to St. Thomas Aquinas
Who gave irrefutable proofs of God's existence and purpose,
I loaded trucks in the garment center.
Me and a black man stole a woman's red dress.
It was of silk; it shimmered.

Upon a gloomy night with all our loving ardors on fire,
We carried it down the long empty avenue,
Each holding one sleeve.
The heat was intolerable causing many terrifying human faces
To come out of hiding.

In the public library reading room
There was a single fan barely turning.
I had the travels of Herman Melville to serve me as a pillow.
I was on a ghost ship with its full sails raised.
I could see no land.
The sea and its monsters could not cool me.

I followed a saintly-looking nurse down a dim hallway.
We edged past people with eyes and ears bandaged.
"I'm a Chinese philosopher in exile,"
I told my landlady that night.
And truly, I no longer looked like myself.
I wore glasses one lens of which had a spider crack.

I stayed in the movies late into the night.
A woman on the screen walked through a bombed city
Again and again. She wore army boots.
Her legs were long and bare. It was cold wherever she was.
Her face was averted, but I was in love with her.
I expected to find wartime Europe at the exit.

It wasn't even snowing. Everyone I met
Had a part of my destiny worn like a mask.
"I'm Bartleby the Scrivener," I told the Italian waiter.
"Me, too," he replied.
And I could see nothing but overflowing ashtrays
The human-faced flies were trying to cross.

from *Antaeus*

GARY SNYDER

Walking the New York Bedrock
Alive in the Sea of Information

◇ ◇ ◇

Maple, oak, poplar, gingko
New leaves, "new green" on a rock ledge
Of steep little uplift, tucked among trees
Hot sun dapple—
                           wake up

Roll over and slide down the rockface
Walk away in the woods toward
A squirrel, toward
Rare people! Seen from a safe distance,
A murmur of traffic approaching,
Siren howls echoing
Through the gridlock of structures,
Vibrating with helicopters,
    the bass tone
Of a high jet.

                    Leap over the park stone wall
                    Dressed fast and light,
                    Slip into the migrating flow

New York like a sea anemone
Wide and waving in the Sea of Economy,
Cadres of educated youth   in chic costume
Step out to the night life, good food, after work

In the chambers of prana-subtle power-pumping
Heartbeat buildings   fired
Deep at the bottom, under the basement.
Fired by old merchant marine
Ex-fire tenders   gone now from sea
To the ships stood on end on the land,
Ex-seamen stand watch at the stationary boilers
    give way to computers,
That monitor heat and the power
Webs underground;   in the air;
In the Sea of Information.

    Keen eyes on the sidewalks,
    Brisk flesh. Beauty and age strut and shuffle

    We curve round the sweep of great corners
    Cardboard chunks tossed up in truckbed
    Delicate jiggle, rouge on the nipple,
    Kohl under the eye.

Time and Life buildings—sixty thousand people—
Wind ripples the banners.
    Stiff shudder shakes limbs on the
    Planted trees growing new green,

Glass, aluminum, aggregate gravel,
Iron. Stainless steel.
Hollow honeycomb brain-buildings owned by

Columbia University, the landlord of
Anemone
        Colony
Alive, in the Sea of Information

"Claus the Wild man"
Lived mostly with Indians,
Was there as a witness when the old lady
"Karacapacomont"
Sold the last bit of Washington Heights, 1701

Down deep grates hear the watercourse,
Rivers that never give up
Trill under the roadbed, over the bedrock
A bird angles way off a brownstone
Couloir that looks like a route,

Echo the hollowing darkness.
Scatter on bedrock, crisscrossing light threads
Gleam sucking squeals up the side streets
One growl shadow
   in an egg of bright lights,
Lick of black on the tongue.
Echoes of sirens come down the walled canyons
Foot lifts to the curb and the lights change—
And look up at the Gods
Equitable god, Celanese god, noble line,
Old Union Carbide god,
Each catching   shares of the squared blocked shadow
Each swinging in sun-dial arc of the day
More than the sum of its parts.
The Guggenheims, the Rockefellers, and the Fricks,
Assembling the art of the world, the plate glass
Window lets light in on "the water lilies"
Like fish or planets, people,
Move, pause, move   through the rooms,
White birch leaves shiver in breezes
While guards watch the world,
Helicopters making their long humming trips

Trading pollen and nectar
In the air
          Of the
Sea of   Economy,

     Drop under the streetworld
     Steel squeal of stopping and starting
     Wind blows through black tunnels
     Spiderwebs, fungus, lichen.

Gingko trees of Gondwanaland. Pictographs,
Petroglyphs, cover the subways—
Empty eye sockets of buildings just built
Soul-less, they still wait the ceremony
     That will make them too,
               New, Big
               City Gods,
Provided with conduit, cable and pipe,
They will light up, breathe cool air,
Breathe the minds of the workers who work there—
The cloud of their knowing
As they soar in the sky, in the air,
Of the Sea
Of Information,

     Cut across alleys and duck beneath trucks.
     "Under Destruction"
     Stop to gaze on the large roman letters
     Of writing on papers that tell of Economy,

Skilsaw whine slips through the windows
Empty room—no walls—such clear air in the cellar
Dry brick, cooked clay, rusty house bodies
Carbide blade skilsaw cuts bricks. Squalls
From the steps leading down to the subway.
Blue-chested runner, a female, on car streets,

Red lights block traffic but she like the
Beam of a streetlight in the whine of the skilsaw,
    She runs right through.

    A cross street leads toward a river
    North returns to the woods
    South takes you fishing
    Peregrines nest at the thirty-fifth floor

Streetpeople rolling their carts
    of whole households
Or asleep wrapped in light blue blanket
    spring evening, at dusk, in a doorway,
Eyeballing arêtes and buttresses rising above them,
    con domus, dominion,
                domus,
    condominate, condominium
Towers,   up there the
Clean crisp white dress white skin
    women and men
Who occupy sunnier niches,
Higher up on the layered stratigraphy cliffs, get
More photosynthesis, flow by more ostracods,
    get more sushi,
Gather more flesh, have delightful
Cascading laughs,

    —Peregrine sails past the window
    Off the edge of the word-chain
    Harvesting concepts, theologies,
    Snapping up bites of the bits bred by
    Banking
        ideas and wild speculations
    On new information—
            and stoops in a blur on a pigeon,

As the street-bottom feeders with shopping carts
Slowly check out the air for the falling of excess,
Of too much, flecks of extra,
From the higher-up folks in the sky

As the fine dusk gleam
　　Lights a whole glass side of
　　Forty some stories
　　Soft liquid silver,

Beautiful buildings we float in, we feed in,

　Foam, steel, gray.

Alive in the Sea of Information.

from *Sulfur*

The Latest Hotel Guest Walks Over Particles That Revolve in Seven Other Dimensions Controlling Latticed Space

◇ ◇ ◇

It is an old established hotel.
She is here for two weeks.
Sitting in the room
toward the end of October,
she turns on three lamps
each with a sixty watt bulb.
The only window opens
on a dark funnel of brick and cement.
Tiny flakes of paint glitter
between the hairs on her arms.
Paint disintegrates from a ceiling
that has surely looked down on the bed beneath it
during World War Two,
the Korean War, Vietnam,
the Cuban Crisis, little difficulties
with the Shah, Covert Action and, presently,
projected Star Wars.
In fact, within that time,
this home away from home, room 404,
probably now contains the escaped molecules,

radiation photons and particulate particles
of the hair and skin of all its former guests.
It would be a kind of queeze mixture of body fluids
and polyester fibers which if assembled,
might be sculptured into an android,
even programmed to weep and beat its head
and shout, "Which war? . . . How much?"
She feels its presence in the dim artificial light.
It is standing in the closet.
There is an obsolete rifle, a bayonet.
It is an anti-hero composed of all the lost nutrinos.
Its feet are bandaged with the lint of old sheets.
It is the rubbish of all the bodies who sweated here.
She hears it among her blouses and slacks
and she knows at this moment it is, at last,
counting from ten to zero.

from *American Poetry Review*

Dummy, 51, to Go to Museum.
Ventriloquist Dead at 75

◇ ◇ ◇

Charlie didn't want to be pushed down
that last time into his plush-lined
case, top hat and monocle removed,
head unscrewed, clever hinge of wooden
jaw detached, the lid snapped shut
and locked, for transmigration to the
Smithsonian. That night, in Bergen's
bedroom, Charlie, in his box, got
himself together by himself and squawked:
"Edgar! You can't make me leave you.
You can't live without me. I'm your
larynx and your tongue. You'd be dumb
without your dummy, Dummy!" Bergen,
stung by that urbane, impudent, bossy,
caustic and beloved voice, silently
swallowed a pearl shirtstud of Charlie's,
spiked with strychnine. Obediently,
Edgar died in his sleep. In the dark
of dislocation, Charlie, glass-eyed, tried

all by himself to weep. A tear of wood
formed and stood in the inner corner
of his left eye, but could not fall.

from *In Other Words*

JAMES TATE

Neighbors

◇ ◇ ◇

Will they have children? Will they have more children?
Exactly what is their position on dogs? Large or small?
Chained or running free? Is the wife smarter than the man?
Is she older? Will this cause problems down the line?
Will he be promoted? If not, will this cause marital stress?
Does his family approve of her, and vice versa? How do
they handle the whole in-law situation? Is it causing some
discord already? If she goes back to work, can he fix
his own dinner? Is his endless working about the yard
and puttering with rain gutters really just a pretext
for avoiding the problems inside the house? Do they still
have sex? Do they satisfy one another? Would he like to
have more, would she? Can they talk about their problems?
In their most private fantasies, how would each of them
change their lives? And what do they think of us, as neighbors,
as people? They are certainly cordial to us, painfully
polite when we chance-encounter one another at the roadside
mailboxes—but then, like opposite magnets, we lunge backward,
back into our own deep root systems, darkness and lust
strangling any living thing to quench our thirst and nourish
our helplessly solitary lives. And we love our neighborhood
for giving us this precious opportunity, and we love our dogs,
our children, our husbands and wives. It's just all so damned
difficult!

from *Sonora Review*

Six of Ox Is

◇　◇　◇

O, no iron, no Rio, no
Red rum murder;
in moon: no omni
devil-lived
derision; no I sired
Otto,
a
drab bard,
Bob,
but no repaid diaper on tub.
O grab me, ala embargo
emit time,
Re-Wop me, empower
Eros' Sore
sinus and DNA sun is
fine, drags as garden if
sad as samara, ruff of fur, a ram; as sad as
Warsaw was raw.

from *New American Writing*

Elsewhere

◊ ◊ ◊

(For Stephen Spender)

Somewhere a white horse gallops with its mane
plunging round a field whose sticks
are ringed with barbed wire, and men
break stones or bind straw into ricks.

Somewhere women tire of the shawled sea's
weeping, for the fishermen's dories
still go out. It is blue as peace.
Somewhere they're tired of torture stories.

That somewhere there was an arrest.
Somewhere there was a small harvest
of bodies in the truck. Soldiers rest
somewhere by a road, or smoke in a forest.

Somewhere there is the conference rage
at an outrage. Somewhere a page
is torn out, and somehow the foliage
no longer looks like leaves but camouflage.

Somewhere there is a comrade,
a writer lying with his eyes wide open
on mattress ticking, who will not read
this, or write. How to make a pen?

And here we are free for a while, but
elsewhere, in one-third, or one-seventh
of this planet, a summary rifle butt
breaks a skull into the idea of a heaven

where nothing is free, where blue air
is paper-frail, and whatever we write
will be stamped twice, a blue letter,
its throat slit by the paper knife of the state.

Through these black bars
hollowed faces stare. Fingers
grip the cross bars of these stanzas
and it is here, because somewhere else

their stares fog into oblivion
thinly, like the faceless numbers
that bewilder you in your telephone
diary. Like last year's massacres.

The world is blameless. The darker crime
is to make a career of conscience,
to feel through our own nerves the silent scream
of winter branches, wonders read as signs.

from *The Arkansas Testament*

ROSANNE WASSERMAN

Inuit and Seal

◇ ◇ ◇

for Gaëtan and Jim

Who has been drinking our air from the other side?
The veils of valentines shake, wind chimes sound, and a hole
  appears
round as a nostril, deep in the lake-blue ice.

One vibration tangibly carries: sky, cobalt glass, blue glaze,
but white petunias swim away from names, alive only so long,
a fabric translucent enough to reflect all shades.

Even when we talk, our garments different shades of rose,
a tone escapes, as if a wooden spear
could not stay in the hand

without concentration,
without becoming
a bundle of sticks and an axe.

But we were bravely talking. How long did it take to form
these rooms, to articulate spaces almost not there?
Hand and eye, back bent, suspense,

and hope: beneath this layer,
a seal might give us sustenance, more than we could believe,
and it rises to breathe just long enough, just so often.

To stay cannily silent that long, till the animal
swims to its highest hunger,
putting its wet snout, warm, to a single accustomed, awaited
   point,

waiting to cry *yes,* never to let
the word break through to shatter
the waiting's end,

we imagine, again,
red rising under blue,
flesh like our own.

                    from *Sulfur*

Respected, Feared, and Somehow Loved

◊ ◊ ◊

In the long run we must fix our compass,
and implore our compass,
and arraign our shadow play in heaven, among the pantheon
where all the plea-bargaining takes place.
                              Within the proscenium arch,
the gods negotiate ceaselessly,
and the words he chooses to express the baleful phrase
            dare to be obsessed
with their instrumentality. Please send for our complete catalogue.

As in the days of creation, the clouds gossip and argue, the gods
            waver.
The gods oversee such unstable criteria as fourthly, fifthly.
The rest are little timbral touches.
The gods waver. To reiterate a point, the gods oversee
the symposium on the life raft—a crazed father, a dead son;
                        an unwarranted curtailment of family.

Part of the foot, and thus part of the grace splinter in dismay,
and the small elite of vitrines where our body parts are stored
dies in a plane crash in Mongolia.
Why didn't someone do something to stop the sins of the climate,
and earlier,

why did not someone rewrite the sins of the vitrines, the windows
shipwrecked icily, the windows called away?

from *O.blēk*

What Memory Reveals

◇ ◇ ◇

Angels, pulled into light—provoking the air, fall
here. You are served a fallow breakfast;
you must stir your juice. Outside, on Columbus Avenue,
a momentary lunge convenes a trafficked burst.

This is not what was intended when they took you to your first
photo session, swaddled. But intent is a ruinous composite.

There were several years of careful steps across
lower Manhattan. A looming sail in a nightmare.
A poolhall, crisscrossed by rudimentary reliefs.
Mayonnaise in a refrigerator door.

You stepped forward, into light, onto a green lawn dotted with
        tumblers
and the hum of Minnesota cicadas. Everywhere a firm rejoinder
        waved.
He whispered the simplest, pettiest of comforts. Your dress alit.

A fat man bends beneath the beaker's proximity.

Freakish, the two that burst into your room where you
were gathering privacy frantically, phonetically.
Burnish (they are flying) regulation (appointments a
calamity of rosewood)—or perhaps they said
furnish the nation. This left a hole, that left a lacking,
and he, the dog, had it, too.

Now Thalia rearranges the glove compartment.
On the right there is a quiet flapping, a whirring
or a wheel joint, in a bright and terrifying night.

It was time that altered monster genes. Pressed to the rear of a
new elevator toward a model apartment, you started with the sail,
with the tremoring that troubles you still. Like the murderer
who only dreamed, you can't shake catastrophe's history.
Your cuff, straightened now, is white against your suit.
The cordialities confirm.

Diving into water his wings conflated. Business
is damage.

What have you pricked, a tourniquet hamstring
under a revolver of lights?

A Lone Ranger replies. There is a waffling like a tournedos
of bundled wings. An egg drops out.

You pay for your breakfast and its litanous menu,
scrambled.
There is earth enough to fill each car,
each open mouth yawing in the light
on Columbus Avenue.

from *Sulfur*

RICHARD WILBUR

Trolling for Blues

◊ ◊ ◊

For John and Barbara

As with the dapper terns, or that sole cloud
Which like a slow-evolving embryo
Moils in the sky, we make of this keen fish
Whom fight and beauty have endeared to us
A mirror of our kind. Setting aside

His unreflectiveness, his flings in air,
The aberration of his flocking swerve
To spawning-grounds a hundred miles at sea,
How clearly, musing to the engine's thrum,
Do we conceive him as he waits below:

Blue in the water's blue, which is the shade
Of thought, and in that scintillating flux
Poised weightless, all attention, yet on edge
To lunge and seize with sure incisiveness,
He is a type of coolest intellect,

Or is so to the mind's blue eye until
He strikes and runs unseen beneath the rip,
Yanking imagination back and down
Past recognition to the unlit deep
Of the glass sponges, of Chiasmodon,

Of the old darkness of Devonian dream,
Phase of a meditation not our own,
That long mêlée where selves were not, that life
Merciless, painless, sleepless, unaware,
From which, in time, unthinkably we rose.

from *Poetry*

ALAN WILLIAMSON

Recitation for the Dismantling of a Hydrogen Bomb

◇ ◇ ◇

From under the flat surface of the planet,
where we know, by statistics, you are waiting,
the White Trains sliding you through our emptiest spaces,
the small grassy doors to you trimly
sunk in the earth by desert or cornfield; then
the neat metal sheath, smaller than a mineshaft, with no
feeling of depth—
                 O how will you ever clearly
come to our sight? Surely our mortal hands
must take you, carry you, do, step by step, the terrible
laying you to sleep, or else— There is no third way.

We have seen you, as in the mirror of a shield,
suddenly standing tall on so many sides of us
like beautiful ghosts—able to hold completely
still on your columns of smoke, then making
a slight lateral tilt to take direction.
And then we realized—everything standing, the rattled
watch on the table a-tick—we were the ghosts,
and you, your power, our inheritors.

And turning from the shield, we saw the world
glare back, withholding; as if a nothingness
already lived in bird and twig, and they
turned their backs on us, to know it.

                                  But our minds
weren't ready yet; they could only wish and wish you
out of this world, out of ourselves.

  We might have thought of sending you
to wander, like a belled goat, the outer space
our fantasies wander so much now, caged
before the dreaming blips of our screens, inventing—
so we are told—a freedom untouched by you.
We would feel the endlessness you were shot into,
in which, if you destroyed,
past the range of our lenses, objects past our knowing,
it would come almost as a lightness, like the sense
of falling that comes before the fall of sleep.
It frees us without cheating you.

                            For we
are grieved to give up a power—as if time
began to run backwards, our bodies shrank and dwindled
until they reached our mothers' wombs, and disappeared.
Some days we'd even rather
use you, and use you up, than live the centuries
you won't quite vanish—the knowledge leaching through us
like your cores buried, after long debate,
in moon-polished canyonlands, always
a mile or so too near a major river . . .

The stars won't hide you. But there are precedents—
if analogy serves still—places
where things too big for us have been sung to sleep
once we knew we couldn't, or no longer wished to,
kill them.

The flesh of death lay on the altar;
—or a class where doctors (the one who speaks a woman,
soft-voiced) teach those in permanent pain to focus
on one word, and cross their legs in the right way,
as if singing, silently, to the thing in themselves . . .

My Lord, good night.

So we set ourselves with sorrow down, to sing to you,
sing you from underground. First, of course, come
the treaties, the surveillance satellite cameras
pinpricking the globe—surface anesthesia
for our tireless fear of each other.

                              Then
it is like taking up hands
against some larger shape of ourselves—the skull-like shield,
the outer fissionable cortex, the inner
strange sky of the lighter-than-air . . . The self-destruct
systems (and the circuits that spoke to them, under the mountains);
the temperatures, equalled only
"in transient phenomena like exploding
supernovae."

              My Lord, good night

                              —our arm
clad with the sun.

Go to sleep in us, as once, they say,
God went to sleep, and we trembled, not only that nothing
any longer overarched us, but that we
must contain what had.

                    (The class is quiet. The doctors
come and go unnoticed, on their beeping
emergency calls. We have gone so far into
what hurts us, whether incalculable nervous twitch

or cancer. Time drifts outside us. Then the voice
—Look at something. Anything. Our eyes open wider
than seemed possible, through blear hospital panes, on things
a little different for each. Brown canyons
of bark. Light combed out past them. End of winter.)

from *American Poetry Review*

Genghis Chan: Private Eye

◊   ◊   ◊

I was floating through a cross section
with my dusty wineglass, when she entered,
a shivering bundle of shredded starlight.
You don't need words to tell a story,
a gesture will do. These days,
we're all parasites looking for a body
to cling to. I'm nothing more
than riffraff splendor drifting past the runway.
I always keep a supply of lamprey lipstick around,
just in case.
                    She laughed,
a slashed melody of small shrugs.
It had been raining in her left eye.
She began: a cloud or story
broken in two maybe four places,
wooden eyelids, and a scarf of human hair.
She paused: I offer you dervish bleakness
and glistening sediment.
                              It was late
and we were getting jammed in deep.

I was on the other side, staring at
the snow covered moon pasted above the park.
A foul lump started making promises in my voice.

from *Sulfur*

Drive, It Said

◇ ◇ ◇

I was in love with a song, kept blurting it out, didn't know the words, maybe something about gazing at stars, I do that too, the constellations like old friends, but I might have been in a hot desert wearing snowshoes, the song would not let me go, I was like someone in love, that was the name of the tune in fact, I played it on the trumpet for the ghost of Kenny Dorham, even missing the highest note out of respect for Kenny's "flat on his ass" style, this song was leading me to something, wasn't it? There was no love in my life, or there *was* love, children are loves, brothers and sisters and old friends are love, even the dog is love, but when the fire in the hearth goes out there's no love, no love served at the table, time to get up, time to leave; my candor is true even if my art is grave. Certainly there was no feeling of new love, no baptismal lifeblood romance excitation stirring up the emotions, the months plodding by, celibate eternities curiously bearable, like an experiment in sensory deprivation these months would go on the soul's résumé, though I didn't feel noble, strong or medieval. Rather sad and exhausted, it's hard to swallow a family, tough to cling to what is no longer there. I could ask for a show of hands here, yes, I could ask for a show of hands.

Hollow at the center of the chest, my lungs, and underneath a shirt, my heart hurt. It was a constant pain, it wasn't painful, it was ponderous, I felt closer to everybody on the street, to the people I didn't know, the disfigured and halt, the guy with the huge goiter on his neck standing with his little dog on the storefront sidewalk, I felt tender toward the scruffy kids in the neighborhood whose fathers were in jail or drunk, people who'd gone through it, or were about to, it hurt to see them, one big unhappy family starring everyone. I was poised on that point where measurement fails, the body clamped in on itself, bruised, the little light pleasures of taste and sound were difficult to endure, hard to put two or three thoughts together, reason through an essay, move from sofa to chair, and back, finally standing up to wolf down a sandwich, single people always eat standing up at the sink, just as love compels me to this dialect, says "take a walk, drive around neighborhood, look at houses," their stiff faces, their colors, their porches, if any, glass in windows divided into panes, smoke from chimneys, formal snowshovels. So much was up in the air, so many moments I'd turn to a last falling leaf, or a dashing cat, and want to speak, say "What's up?" or "Where are the boys?" Elements of an unraveling tale written by squirrels in the circular sockets of a brain, I was eager for duties, for the demands of a job, contact with real people around a real table, I am literal, lived in, to think out loud is not to say much until it's written, give me a life in turmoil so I can feel what size brushstrokes will convey its portrait, the set of jaw, eyes the way the painter saw them, slipping. Homemade tapes accompanied my long commutes, driving was music, music never sounded more fundamental, like a dictionary come alive, it entered bodily, it was purposeful direction, all touch and go. I didn't know any teenage girls flipping out, didn't have to include that sound, sometimes silence and the humming car would take on the shape of domestic anger's impossible heavy life injustice, no one to blame, not even myself, or the culture, a vicious spear thrust into the shell of the alien other, it hit me, I closed up around it, a sea anemone. Why do we hold on to the pain, perform heroic measures to sustain an embalmed identity? Why not melt into it and notice a seagull's beak?

Or I would begin to flirt with desire for the very change I feared, to be free of the rasps, to be on my own again, be my own boss, make my own clichés, hang my own pictures, dial my own information, less security, but more adventure, less friction, more desire, click the lights off, knock back the heat and slip upstairs to read late into the night, a light that disturbs no one, a few pillows behind the back, a notebook on the nightstand, you can see me here, I'm covered from head to toe, it's an 18th-Century classic, it's a copy of *Tears on My Pillow*, it's the neo-wave of the present, I'm wide awake, there's so much to read, so many sentences to speak out loud, words to prowl.

The bedside clock ticks, it's a different tune, it sings, "Take care of yourself and get plenty of rest," then sleep like a sponge drops, sops up awareness, involuntary muscular jerks unkink the self, a distant voice whispers, "Take the night off, Lonesome. You can't just have these emotions, you gotta pay for 'em." I was like someone in love falling asleep alone, but only like, there was no one there but memory, but fear, cold mornings the sun would tip through the east facing windows and arrive on my skin all but extinguished, the light bouncing off the snow was a screaming vitamin, and curious people would tour the little house, it was amusing, I didn't own it, things began to fill it, tables on loan, sofa too, I'd be self-conscious, apologize for the bow in the shelves containing the poetry books, made 'em myself, the rooms so small my eyes could travel the spines, I could jump out of bed and reach a volume of my choice and be back under the covers before the mattress knew I'd left. Sometimes I think everything I know I've learned from poems, then I wake up, I see whole rooms exactly as they were, filled with paintings, I think I'm still in them, the Malevitch room at the Stedelyk in Amsterdam, it's a space-station on the trajectory of abstract painting, I sit back down and watch it orbit, it's supreme.

My dreams these mornings weren't spectacular, some revenge, some lust, but the big gnawing fact relentless and obsessive was there to greet me at dawn, a broken record, a tapeloop, in the video version the fact planted its green flag in my face, I was its imagery's victim, even as the credits went rolling by, our distant vows went back into the can for the next night's showing, beginning middle and end, finito, history, join the club. I bought a TV set and played the remote buttons like a thumb piano, it broke the silence, it lit the walls, and at dusk I'd say to myself, as I reached for the lamp, "Light the first light of evening," in stentorian tones, or "His gorgeous self-pity." So much for darkness then, but the darkness was only more apparent in the lamplight, I couldn't see where I was going, the body, my own, the room like a cage, moving from chair to sofa, legs tucked up under for warmth, a blanket, a magazine, I was 85 years old, I was fifteen, a manuscript was my afghan, a pile of mail, then the hop-up adrenaline of a phone call, let's have another show of hands here, you've been there too, it's ringing just for you, the miniscule bag of groceries, silent rice, passing moments passing, sponged whiteness of stove, sink, all the books filed away, the rug unwalked on, records in alphabetical order, a new ribbon, a stack of envelopes, the liquid paper crust that fell as white dots swept into the trash, I was puttering, not paralyzed, I was waiting, I remembered hitchhiking through Bulgaria with a Lebanese guy in a two-door sedan, and stopping to share cigarettes in a village off the main road. People suddenly materialized, we were surrounded, they looked at our clothes, we exchanged furtive smiles, kidded with the children, then out of nowhere a woman advances, hands us a just-baked loaf of bread, it's big and round and solid and warm and we are immediately touched, we thank them, I shake the woman's hand, it is callused and rough, her eyes are light brown, they are filled with amber lines that seem to spin, while my hands are soft, I'm bookish, I'll sleep tonight on the floor of the train station in Sofia, use my bookbag for a pillow, be up early fully dressed still and away, is there still a crust of that bread? Later picked up in Yugoslavia by a Persian driving a truckload of rugs to Munich, you want to hear about this guy? I believe my senses, I finally had to escape from him in Vienna, completely unstrung me, he was single-minded devotion, we shared five words in English and that's all. One night at a truck stop outside Belgrade, about midnight of a moonless starry night, we stopped to eat, he propositioned our blond waitress, we finished the meal, and she followed us out to the truck, got in between us, we drove a mile down the road, pitchblack. He pulled to the side and stopped. He grabbed a blanket from the cab, they got out, they disappeared into the featureless landscape. Is this the freebooting life of adventure so ably described in the *Tropic of Cancer*? Was I next? Could one say No, in Serbo-Croatian? Is there a God? I can't see them out there. Then just as suddenly as the truck had stopped, and they'd gotten out, she was back, alone, she was furious, she grabbed her jacket from the cab, she was livid, her light summer dress fit her perfectly, she slammed the cab door and took off walking down the highway, back to her truck stop. What had my Persian rug trucker done to earn her disapproval? It was a precipitate disaster. He got back to the truck, threw the blanket in the cab, shrugged his shoulders, and off we drove into the night, there were borders to cross, spring floodwaters rushing off the Alps to admire. But by the time we got to Vienna, after some harrowing driving routines in dense traffic, some lane-changing leaps of faith that only a true son of Allah's compassionate protection could have gotten away with, he finally pulled off onto a side street, it was about 8 o'clock, we stopped, he said, "Girls" (that was one of the five words we shared) and smiled, reached under the front seat, brought out a razor, a mug with soap, a brush, some cold water from a bottle, and a filthy hand towel, and proceeded to lather up the soap for his evening shave, daubing cold water on his bristly dark beard, and glancing over at me as if to indicate, What an Evening We'll Have! But listening to him pull that dull razor across his cold scraped cheeks I nearly gagged, he was really scraping, nicking chin and cheek, his towel on the seat I wouldn't even touch. I had to cut, jam, no time to get sick, I thanked him for the lift, he looked surprised, I was abandoning him! Where was my sense of fun? I grabbed my bag, opened the cab door, swung down, waved once, and took off walking down the city street, it was meant to be, back on my own two feet, and all aboard for the night train to Munich, I was on it, now it's the next day, it's two in the afternoon and I've just eaten a bratwurst and drunk a beer, I turn a corner and nearly bump into the only person I know in all of Germany, a girlfriend named Brigitte Gapp with a Marilyn Monroe–like birthmark on a pale cheek, dark hair, big bright smile, I go crazy, this is serendipity writ large, Jung's magic synchronicity, we fall into each other's arms, we stare, the only person I know, how account for it? The mind entertains a wisdom that the body can't understand.

People would say it takes a year, maybe two, there was money on the table, there were things, what was spoiled needed division, a few rounds of letterhead legality meetings on creamy stationery, the feints and dodges, the disclosures, the aggressive silence, the screaming meemies, the three-piece options expert, the comma that allows, insists, demands another term, something must follow the end of the world, this one here, the oil burner clicks on, these words cost money, it was happening to other people too, it was commonplace, you could join a group and discuss it, commiserating phone calls from old friends long since lost track of, the word spreads, a postcard from a woman in New York wanting to meet, we've mutual friends, let's have a drink, there's one in Stockbridge, you could drive down together, a movie nut uptown, I'd really like her, the chorus chorused, she's just breaking up with, this is the network speaking, it's an erotic universe of random strangers coupling, the matchmakers were lighting up, they closed the cover before striking, life could resume, don't hesitate, change your sheets, act like someone in love would act, get that bounce back into your step, kid, talk funny again, and all so nice and young. *Quel* sequence. It's typical though isn't it? There's more variety in a crisis, more sense of drama in the pain of a social hello, to be on the crest of a breaking wave, but would you get smashed to the sand and ground up, or ride it for all it's worth into a new life, stolen like fire from the gods one burning finger at a time? Drive, it said, digitalized, accessed, therapied, the talk in every cafe on Main Street. This is our human universe, the glue on a chipped cup, this end that signals a new beginning is the cheapest gas in town. I drink it myself.

from *New American Writing*

CONTRIBUTORS' NOTES AND COMMENTS

A. R. AMMONS was born in Whiteville, North Carolina, in 1926. He attended Wake Forest College and did graduate work at Berkeley. He has received the National Book Award (1973), the Bollingen prize (1975), the National Book Critics Circle Award (1981), and a MacArthur Prize Fellowship. His most recent books are *The Selected Poems: Expanded Edition* and *Sumerian Vistas*, both published by Norton in 1987. He has taught at Cornell University since 1964.

Of "Motion Which Disestablishes Organizes Everything," Ammons writes: "When poems get too skinny and bony, emaciated nearly into left-hand margin, so highly articulated their syllables crystallize, I go back to long lines to loosen up, to blur the issues of motion into minor forms within larger motions. I believe something like that was taking place some three or four years ago when I wrote this poem and three or four others like it."

RALPH ANGEL, born in Seattle, Washington, in 1951, is an associate professor of English at the University of Redlands, California, where he teaches creative writing. *Anxious Latitudes* is his first major collection of poetry (Wesleyan University Press, 1986). "Shadow Play" and two other recent poems were awarded *Poetry* magazine's 1987 Bess Hokin Prize.

Angel writes: " 'Shadow Play' was loosely inspired by the *wayang kulit*, the sacred shadow-puppet plays of Indonesia. In the shadow theater, the audience does not look directly at the flat-image puppets but rather views their shadows, which are projected onto a translucent screen. The puppet master can be interpreted as the high priest, the projected shadows as souls, and the screen as heaven."

RAE ARMANTROUT lives in San Diego. She has published three books of poems: *Extremities* (The Figures, 1978), *The Invention of Hunger* (Tuumba, 1979), and *Precedence* (Burning Deck, 1985). Her poems have recently appeared in such anthologies as *In the American Tree* (National Poetry Foundation, 1986) and *Language Poetries* (New Directions, 1987). She teaches at the University of California at San Diego.

Armantrout writes: " 'Bases' is a sometimes (or loosely) narrative poem concerning bases for comparison, bases for belief. Written during the Iran-Contra scandal, when public duplicity was very apparent, it combines materials from public and private realms. To an extent, I think, 'Bases' demonstrates the pervasive climate of suspicion and doubt engendered by political events."

JOHN ASH was born in Manchester, England, in 1948. He has lived in New York City since the fall of 1985. He has published five books: *Casino* (Oasis Books, 1978), *The Bed* (Oasis Books, 1981), *The Goodbyes* (Carcanet, 1982), *The Branching Stairs* (Carcanet, 1985), and, most recently, *Disbelief* (Carcanet, 1987).

Ash writes: "I thought of 'Memories of Italy' as a 'broken sestina' until someone pointed out that it is a quintuple fugue. It is as purely 'musical' as anything written in words can be. Or so I like to think. The poems 'From a High Place' and 'Little Variations for Natalia Ginzburg' (both in *Disbelief*) employ similar techniques."

JOHN ASHBERY, the guest editor of *The Best American Poetry, 1988*, was born in Rochester, New York, in 1927. He is the author of twelve books of poetry, including *April Galleons* (Viking, 1987). Twice named a Guggenheim Fellow, he received the Pulitzer Prize, the National Book Award, and the National Book Critics Circle Award for his 1975 collection *Self-Portrait in a Convex Mirror* (Viking). A volume of his art criticism, *Reported Sightings*, is to be published in 1989 by Knopf.

TED BERRIGAN (1934–1983) was born in Providence, Rhode Island, moved to New York City in the early 1960s, and became a key figure in the second generation of the New York School of poetry. Berrigan's books of poetry include *The Sonnets* (Grove, 1964), *Noth-*

ing for You (United Artists, 1978), and *So Going Around Cities: New and Selected Poems, 1958–1979* (Blue Wind, 1980). He was the editor of *C* magazine in the 1960s, and taught at Yale, Iowa City, and elsewhere. His posthumous collection, *A Certain Slant of Sunlight*, is forthcoming from O Books in 1988.

Edited by the poet Alice Notley (who was married to Berrigan), *A Certain Slant of Sunlight* includes Berrigan's "postcard poems" —such as "My Autobiography"—which he wrote on blank postcards in 1982. In a headnote to a dozen of these poems published in *New American Writing* in 1987, Notley writes that "the postcard-poem form influences the poet toward direct address to individuals; epigram; thievery (there being so many cards to fill); & a search for new shapes. Also, you could write a previously written poem of yours, by writing it on a postcard; now it was part of your new book! Finally, this was a remarkably social writing project—lines & words & pictures being often provided by friends, drop-ins, & etceteras, as well as dead poets in books & in mind. . . . There are about a hundred & fifty more." Notley's latest book of poems is *At Night the States* (Yellow Press).

MEI-MEI BERSSENBRUGGE was born in Beijing in 1947, and grew up in Massachusetts. She lives in New Mexico and in Providence, Rhode Island, with her husband, the artist Richard Tuttle. Her recent books are *The Heat Bird* (Burning Deck, 1983) and *Empathy* (Station Hill).

Berssenbrugge writes: " 'Chinese Space' is inspired by a floor plan my mother drew for me, of the house where I was born in Beijing, and includes bits of family history. It wants to explore the experience of space across time as a metaphor for the interaction of memory and identity."

GEORGE BRADLEY was born in Roslyn, New York, in 1953. His work has appeared in many magazines, including *The New Yorker, Poetry, The Paris Review, Shenandoah, Antaeus, Partisan Review, American Poetry Review, The Yale Review,* and *The New Republic. Terms to Be Met,* his collection of poems, was published in the Yale Younger Poets Series in 1986. He lives in New York City.

Of *"Noch Einmal, an Orpheus,"* Bradley writes: "I suppose this poem started with the rather banal idea of performing a pun upon the word *revision*. It seemed that Orpheus's famous backward glance might be understood not only as an example of the human at a loss in the realm of the supernatural, but also as an error characteristic of a poet. Or better, that the poet's habitual activity is only another testimony to human nature. Of course, when one writes a poem about Orpheus, it is a great temptation to do so in a sonnet. Perhaps it was one that ought to have been resisted, since I'm not sure anyone can get away scot-free with a 'Sonnet to Orpheus' anymore. Oh, well, one of the first rules of poetry is that if a thing is worth doing to begin with, it has to be done again and again and again."

STEFAN BRECHT was born in 1924, served in the U.S. Army (1944–45), and received a Ph.D. (1957). His *Poems* was published by Lawrence Ferlinghetti (City Lights, 1978). His third book (in two volumes) of a series titled The Original Theatre of the City of New York is forthcoming from Methuen. He lives in Manhattan and in Sandisfield, Massachusetts.

JOSEPH BRODSKY received the Nobel Prize for literature in 1987. Exiled from the Soviet Union in 1972, he came to settle in the United States and now lives in New York City. His collections of poems include *A Part of Speech* (1980) and the forthcoming *To Urania*, both from Farrar, Straus & Giroux. *Less than One* (Farrar, Straus & Giroux), his collection of essays, was published in 1986 and won the National Book Critics Circle Award for criticism.

NICHOLAS CHRISTOPHER was born in 1951 in New York City, where he now lives, and was educated at Harvard College. He is the author of two books of poems, *On Tour with Rita* (Knopf, 1982) and *A Short History of the Island of Butterflies* (Viking, 1986). In 1986–87 he was awarded poetry fellowships by the National Endowment for the Arts and the New York Foundation for the Arts. His new book is *Desperate Characters, a Novella in Verse and Other Poems* (Viking Penguin, 1988).

Of "Miranda in Reno," Christopher writes: "At the time I wrote this poem, I was working on a long narrative poem—actually, a 'novella in verse,' as it was subsequently subtitled—called *Desperate*

Characters. Most of my poems are lyric poems, and despite the fact I had written a number of shorter narrative poems, and even a novel, composing a one-hundred-page poem was a very different undertaking. While wrestling with the inherent musical and tensive demands of poetry, I was juggling characters, dialogue, geography, historical and philosophical motifs, and a 'plot,' charted for the most part in the charged terrain of my characters' overlapping psyches.

"All of which is to say that 'Miranda in Reno,' like the other lyric poems I wrote around *Desperate Characters*, emerged as a dramatic monologue in which the narrator speaks through the filter of her dreams and putative reality around a central theme. In retrospect, I see that all these poems (written in clusters: there were three 'Miranda' poems) were perhaps offshoots of the long poem. They are different from one another thematically, but each seems to reflect some aspect of, or variation on, the numerous voices I was employing in the long poem. The specific genesis of 'Miranda in Reno' I remember quite clearly: a file card on which I wrote the first line, and then a month later jotted, in parentheses, the quote from Schopenhauer (which I had read some years ago) that would begin stanza 3 when the poem came to me in its entirety two months later."

MARC COHEN was born in Brooklyn, New York, in 1951. He received his M.F.A. in creative writing at Brooklyn College in 1975. His poems have appeared in such magazines as *Shenandoah, Partisan Review,* and *Verse,* and in the anthology *Ecstatic Occasions, Expedient Forms* (Collier Books, 1988). For the past twelve years he has worked for a manufacturer of office filing equipment in Brooklyn. He lives in New York City.

Of "Mecox Road," Cohen writes: "This narrative poem was conceived during a summer visit to the painter Darragh Park's home in Bridgehampton, New York. I was sitting on the porch with Darragh and some friends, including Darragh's lurcher, Oriane. The pond and the bench that appear in the poem are clearly visible from the porch; Darragh has a separate studio on the property. The landscape moved me, as did a visit to Darragh's studio later that day. A few days later, I recollected the experience in tranquility.

"At the beginning of the poem, the narrator, who must evoke meaning through objects, appears to be set against the painter, who evokes color through objects. Although moved by the surroundings, the narrator stands apart from them—and becomes convinced, by the poem's end, that 'color' is more important than 'meaning.' The opposite effect from Williams's 'no ideas but in things' has taken place. What the bench represents becomes more important than the bench itself; there are 'no things but in ideas,' and the sum total of all the ideas presented becomes the made object, the poem itself. The narrator discovers, too, that he is part of nature, not separate from it."

WANDA COLEMAN was born and raised in the Watts section of Los Angeles. She now lives in Hollywood and makes her living as a medical secretary/transcriber. Formerly a dancer with Anna Halprin's Dancers' Workshop (*Ceremony of Us*) in San Francisco, she received a literary fellowship from the National Endowment for the Arts in 1981 and a Guggenheim Fellowship in 1984. She is a cohost of "The Poetry Connexion," an interview program on Southern California's Pacifica radio station. Black Sparrow Press has published three of her books—*Mad Dog Black Lady* (1979), *Imagoes* (1983), and *Heavy Daughter Blues* (1987)—and will publish her first collection of fiction, *A War of Eyes*.

Of "Essay on Language," Coleman writes: "Near as I can tell, the literary game is no different from the commercial writing game—game is game, which is all my 'essay' is 'about' (if it's game one is after)."

CLARK COOLIDGE was born in Providence, Rhode Island, in 1939. He has lectured at the Naropa Institute in Boulder, Colorado, and at New College of California in San Francisco, and he was a writer-in-residence at the American Academy in Rome, 1984–85. Recent books include *Solution Passage (Poems 1978–1981)* (Sun & Moon Press, 1986), *The Crystal Text* (The Figures, 1986), *Mesh* (In Camera), *At Egypt* (The Figures), and *Sound as Thought (Poems 1982–1984)* (Sun & Moon Press).

Coolidge writes: " 'A Monologue' was written in June of 1981. I'd been reading Pinter's plays. And Beckett's work, of course (his

A Piece of Monologue had appeared). No doubt Michael Palmer's radio plays (*IDEM 1–4*) were on my mind as well. I had written *6 Dialogues* around the same time. Potential here for other voices in further play, as yet unwritten."

ALFRED CORN was born in Georgia in 1943. He is the author of five books of poetry published by Viking Penguin. The poem printed here is from his most recent collection, *The West Door*, which appeared early in 1988. Recently named a Fellow of the Academy of American Poets, Corn lives in New York City and teaches at the Graduate School of the Arts at Columbia University. *The Metamorphoses of Metaphor*, a collection of his critical writings, was published in 1987 by Viking.

DOUGLAS CRASE was born in 1944 in Battle Creek, Michigan, grew up on a farm, and went to Princeton University. He is the author of *The Revisionist* (Little, Brown, 1981) and has been awarded a Guggenheim Fellowship, a Whiting Writer's Award, and the Witter Bynner Prize for poetry from the American Academy and Institute of Arts and Letters. In 1987, he was named a MacArthur Fellow. He lives in New York City.

Crase writes: "In 'Dog Star Sale,' the spare punctuation seems fit for conclusions so obviously provisional—though I guess if you turned that into a general principle it would make punctuation everywhere the exception rather than the rule. The Dog Star, Sirius, has a white dwarf companion that accounts for the wobble in its proper motion. A poem, too, can have an obscure companion that makes it wobble, and sometimes this will be its subject. One July 23rd I went into a store where they were holding a one-day sale because it was the date when the Dog Star first rises in the dawn sky. It had not occurred to me so forcefully until then that not just North America, but the universe, would be for sale."

ROBERT CREELEY was born in Arlington, Massachusetts, in 1926. At Black Mountain College, where he taught between 1954 and 1956, he established and edited *Black Mountain Review*. Since 1966, he has taught at the State University of New York at Buffalo, where he now holds the Gray Chair Professorship in poetry. His recent books include *Memory Gardens* (New Directions, 1986) and *The Collected Poems of Robert Creeley, 1945–1975* (University of California Press, 1983).

Of "The Dream," Creeley writes: "The poem was provoked by conversation with a genial Freudian analyst, who, when I'd completed my telling of this dream, said, 'You must never quite get what you want . . . ' "

TOM DISCH was born in Des Moines, Iowa, in 1940. He is the author of *The Businessman: A Tale of Terror* (Harper & Row, 1984) and *Camp Concentration*, novels; *Getting into Death*, short stories (Knopf, 1976); *The Brave Little Toaster*, a children's book (Doubleday, 1986); and *Amnesia* (Electronic Arts, San Mateo, Calif., 1986), a computer interactive novel. His collections of poetry include *Burn This* (1982) and *Here I Am, There You Are, Where Were We* (1984), both from Hutchinson. He reviews plays for *The Nation* and is on the board of directors of the National Book Critics Circle. He lives in New York City.

KENWARD ELMSLIE was born in New York City in 1929. His books include *26 Bars* (tales), *The Orchid Stories* (Doubleday, 1973) (a novel), *Motor Disturbance* (Columbia University Press, 1971), *Tropicalism* (Z Press, 1976), and *Moving Right Along* (Z Press, 1980) (poetry), and *The Seagull, Lizzie Borden*, and *Three Sisters* (opera librettos). A singing poet, he appeared off-off-Broadway in a cabaret revue of his songs, *Palais Bimbo*, in 1987. His most recent albums are *Palais Bimbo Lounge Show* and *26 Bars*, a cassette. His play *City Junket* was produced off-Broadway.

Elmslie writes: " 'Top O' Silo' was inspired by my collaborator, Donna Dennis, who created drawings for *26 Bars,* an alphabet work about drinking establishments. This particular tale evolved out of the drawing, which came first—and also memories of time Donna had spent in South Dakota creating an installation, a tourist cabin half-submerged in a river. As I'd just polished off several dense multivoiced tales for our book, I relished the chance to work out a simpler narrative, rooted and not floaty, with disturbing underpinnings barely present—a calmed-down good-natured version of my own deep dread of being trapped in a flat heartland forever."

ALICE FULTON was born in Troy, New York, in 1952. Her first book of poems, *Dance Script with Electric Ballerina,* won the 1982 Associated Writing Programs Award and was published by the University of Pennsylvania Press in 1983. Her second book, *Palladium* (University of Illinois Press, 1986), won the 1985 National Poetry Series and the 1987 Society of Midland Authors Award. Her poems, essays, and reviews have appeared in *The New Yorker, Poetry, The Yale Review, Ploughshares, The Georgia Review,* and in the anthology *Ecstatic Occasions, Expedient Forms* (Collier Books, 1988). She has been a Fellow of the Provincetown Fine Arts Work Center, the Michigan Society of Fellows, and the Guggenheim Foundation. She is the William Wilhartz Assistant Professor of English at the University of Michigan, Ann Arbor.

Of "Losing It," Fulton writes: " 'Losing It' describes and reenacts a near-death experience, the loss of consciousness and memory, from the viewpoint of the recovered victim. You'll notice that the last line in stanza two ('When your brain's become a Byzantine cathedral . . .') and all of stanza three are repeated later in the poem. I wanted readers to have a sensation of déjà vu upon reading these words a second time. The repetition is mimetic in that reliving the past is one of memory's functions. And having the words return in slightly altered form mirrors the revisionary (or unintentionally slippery) aspect of memory. The first time these lines appear, the speaker (and the reader) believe that loss of consciousness has been accurately captured in language. The second time around, it's evident that the image is a created construct, something imagined in retrospect, an order placed upon a terrifying experience and not the experience itself. At this point the speaker's faith, which depends upon expressing experience through language, begins to erode.

"Describing non-being is a contradiction in terms. In making the attempt, we rely on concrete images, metaphors, things we can perceive with the senses. The flood of elaborate, dense language creates a context of contrast for the stanza beginning 'Then you discard the flood.' At this point, the poem shifts to the first person and the language opens up and becomes less clotted. The speaker briefly lost the power to describe and remember; all she had was an engulfing nothing. Now she grasps at non-words like *ne, ex, un* to give it voice. You could say her attempt to capture the absence of consciousness begins in eloquence and comes to grunts. Her defenses crumbled, she again turns to memory, recalling the death of her aunt. Watching 'From the high ground of health / and self-control' as her aunt died was an unbearable experience, one that made her want to forget herself and beg, to depend again on those inarticulate bits of scream and groan that fill us when prayers fail. Ultimately, even memory does not afford control or consolation so much as it enforces knowledge of all (aunt, memory, self, matter) she and we must lose."

AMY GERSTLER was born in San Diego, California, in 1956. Her seven published books include *The True Bride* (Lapis Press, 1986) and *Primitive Man* (Hanuman, 1987). In 1987 she won second prize in *Mademoiselle* magazine's fiction contest. She has taught sign language and remedial reading and is now assistant director of Beyond Baroque Literary/ Arts Center, a nonprofit arts organization in Venice, California. She lives in Los Angeles.

Of "Marriage," Gerstler writes: "The line that is repeated ('I kiss you. I do') is lifted from an intensely lovely Godard film about the Virgin Mary, and other lines are borrowed or pilfered (and then let alone or bent) from other sources."

JORIE GRAHAM teaches at the University of Iowa Writers' Workshop. She is the author of three collections of poems: *Hybrids of Plants and of Ghosts* (1980), *Erosion* (1983), both published by Princeton University Press, and *The End of Beauty* (Ecco Press, 1987).

DEBORA GREGER teaches in the creative writing program of the University of Florida. Two collections of her poems have been published by Princeton University Press: *Movable Islands* (1980) and *And* (1986). She has received grants from the National Endowment for the Arts (1978 and 1985), the John Simon Guggenheim Memorial Foundation (1987), and the Ingram Merrill Foundation (1981). She has also been awarded a Mary Ingraham Bunting Fellowship (1980), an Amy Lowell Traveling Poetry Scholarship (1981), and a Peter I. B. Lavan Younger Poets Award from the Academy of American Poets (1987).

ALLEN GROSSMAN is the author of six books of poetry, of which the most recent are *The Woman on the Bridge Over the Chicago River* (1979), *Of the Great House* (1982), and *The Bright Nails Scattered on the Ground* (1986), all published by New Directions. His views on poetry may be found in *Against Our Vanishing* (Rowan Tree, 1981). He teaches at Brandeis University.

Of "The Piano Player Explains Himself," Grossman writes: "God may create everything (alas!), but persons must not. To 'play the piano' is to reduce the splendor of the music (His music) in accord with the imperfect powers of the human maker—as to *write* a poem is to reduce the inhuman forces of which it is the trace to the human form of their saying, in accord with the blessed laws of our imperfection which the poet knows. We have in *mind* an unplayed instrument which defines our nature by exhausting it. That instrument must be taken in hand because it can only be taken in hand for what the hand can do.

"Thus 'The Piano Player Explains Himself' is about the purpose for which the poet (the piano player in the poem) takes in hand his instrument. The purpose for which the poet must, despite all, keep on saying his say is the regulation of the forces of mind and world—not in themselves human, as we see everywhere about us. The instrument of the poet is no other than the great Laws of his practice. In the reality of the poem (which is the world in which we live) the instrument is unplayed and yet remains to be played, like the piano in a middle-class living room which no one alive can play and no one can remove—or like a power of mind capable of overcoming the violence of mind, to which the poet (perhaps the poet alone) has access by reason of his knowledge of the poetic instrument.

"As for the Lady, she is the sign of the force (in all its dark and numinous beauty) for which the music of the Law secures the human form—the *fashion* of the person. The wind is from the direction of fair weather (North, and North by West). Through death after death her lover grows more powerful in her service, as the formal courtesy of the poem intends to exemplify."

BARBARA GUEST lives in New York City. Her poetry collections include *The Blue Stairs* (Corinth, 1968), *The Countess from Minne-*

apolis (Burning Deck, 1976), *Moscow Mansions* (Viking, 1973). She is the author of a novel, *Seeking Air* (Black Sparrow, 1978). Her most recent publications are a biography of H.D., *Herself Defined* (Doubleday, 1984), and a book of poems, *Fair Realism* (Sun & Moon Press).

Of "Words," Guest writes: "The poem was composed by positioning a succession of words upon the doorstep of that mysterious realm where a poem's promised dust is laid.

"I am amused to have a 'semiotic' aspect reported, like a memorable distant halo, and believe that were I to entitle the poem this moment I would call it 'Spoons.' "

RACHEL HADAS is the author of three books of poems (most recently *A Son from Sleep*, published by Wesleyan University Press in 1987) and a book of criticism on Frost's and Seferis's use of landscape imagery. Her poems, essays, and reviews have appeared in *The Yale Review*, *The Threepenny Review*, and *Partisan Review*. She teaches English at the Newark campus of Rutgers University and likes to tell her students that she managed to avoid majoring in English, since her degrees are in classics and comparative literature. She lives in New York City with her husband and son.

Of "Nourishment," Hadas writes: " 'Nourishment' is one of 19 poems written in a manic burst at the MacDowell Colony in January 1987. At the kind of distance from my own life that that blessed place provides, I was able to scoop up all sorts of disparate ingredients. The drained arm in stanza three, for example, appeared in a dream I had, early in my stay, about donating nearly transparent blood; in fact, soon before leaving the city I had given blood, and I'd certainly felt that my life as mother/ teacher/ poet was bleeding me white. The long spoon and italicized cajolings of the first stanza are skimmed from a poem-in-progress by a fellow colonist that seemed, as she read it, to be pledging eternal devotion to a completely unresponsive mate.

"There's a literary antecedent to 'Nourishment'; I had George Herbert's incomparable 'Love III,' with its table set for two, at the back of my mind as I wrote. My husband George Edwards, a composer, had been setting this and other Herbert poems to music at MacDowell the previous winter; and I had Herbert's deceptively placid tone, his domestic imagery, and the strong push and pull of his long and short lines in my ear and eye.

"My poem is about finding a path to a house and sitting down to a silent meal. I suppose it's a meditation on marriage, cast into a mildly narrative meander constrained by stanzaic boundaries. The rhythm which I hope these boundaries both control and intensify is that of the lifeblood pumping, nourishing not thirsty ghosts but the living work."

DONALD HALL, who is officially New Hampshire's poet laureate, was interviewed on TV a lot during the week of the New Hampshire primary in 1988. Hall writes: "I live in a New Hampshire house where my grandmother and my mother were born. I taught at a university for thirteen years, then in 1975 quit my job for freelance writing. I support myself by poetry readings and by writing articles in magazines, juveniles, textbooks, plays, short stories, and biography. First thing in the day I work on poems. The last two books have been *Kicking the Leaves* (Harper & Row, 1978) and *The Happy Man* (Random House, 1986), which won the Lenore Marshall/Nation Award."

Of "Prophecy," Hall writes: 'Prophecy' is one of 'Four Classic Texts' (together with 'Pastoral,' 'History,' and 'Eclogue') that make the middle of a long poem, *The One Day*, which Ticknor & Fields will publish in September 1988. The whole poem began in the fall of 1971, when I was subject to long and frequent attacks of language. I wrote as rapidly as I could write, page after page, loose free verse characterized by abundance and strangeness rather than by anything else, certainly not by art. After a month or two the onslaught stopped. Every now and then over the next few years, lines would occur that announced themselves as part of this work. In 1979 and 1980 I tried to find a form. In 1981 the poem began to shape itself.

"Not that I knew what I was doing. If *The One Day* (or 'Prophecy') is intended, it is intended by not being crossed out. I wrote with excitement but without judgment; afterwards I concentrated to decide whether to keep what I wrote down. If it succeeds, this poem is impulse validated by attention."

ROBERT HASS is the author of *Field Guide* (Yale University Press, 1973) and *Praise* (Ecco Press, 1979). He has also published a book of essays, *Twentieth Century Pleasures: Prose on Poetry* (Ecco Press, 1984), which was awarded the National Book Critics Circle prize in criticism. He lives in Berkeley, California, and teaches nearby at St. Mary's College of California in Moraga.

Hass writes: "I don't know what to say about 'Thin Air.' It was written in the summer in the Sierra Nevada mountains, where mule ears are the most common high meadow vegetation. Their leaves prick up, curiously or hopefully, and have begun to wilt and dry out by late August. The poem was written in a rush, and then again, later, more slowly."

SEAMUS HEANEY was born in County Derry, Northern Ireland, in 1939. He taught at Queens University, Belfast, before leaving Northern Ireland in 1972. His books of poetry include *Death of a Naturalist*, (Faber & Faber, 1966), *Wintering Out*, (Oxford University Press, 1972), *North* (Faber & Faber, 1975), *Field Work* (1979), *Station Island* (1985), and *The Haw Lantern* (1987), the last three published by Farrar, Straus & Giroux. A gathering of his prose writings was published under the title *Preoccupations* (Farrar, Straus & Giroux, 1980). He lives in Dublin and spends part of the year in the United States, where he teaches at Harvard University.

ANTHONY HECHT was born in New York City in 1923. He has taught at several universities, including the University of Rochester, New York, and now lives in Washington, D.C., where he is University Professor at Georgetown University. His first book of poetry was *A Summoning of Stones* (Macmillan, 1954). *The Hard Hours* (Atheneum, 1967) won the Pulitzer Prize for 1968. His most recent books are *The Venetian Vespers* (1979), a collection of poems, and a prose collection titled *Obbligati: Essays in Criticism* (1985), both from Atheneum.

Of "Envoi," Hecht writes: "In my childhood the radio comedian Fred Allen used occasionally to play the role of a Chinese sleuth named 'One Long Pan,' who, in what was supposed characteristically to be an Oriental handicap, was unable to pronounce r's, and would in consequence raise gales of audience hilarity (probably dubbed) by his pronunciation of *revolver,* always the fatal weapon, as *lewallawa.* (In actual fact, it seems not to be *r*'s but *l*'s that Asian-Americans have difficulty with in speaking Western languages, so that Allen's detective would probably have pronounced his name, 'One Wrong Pan.') The frisbee tossers on today's campuses are deft enough almost to make you believe that it's UFOs they're handling, and the Japanese might almost be small and ingenious enough to fit inside them. In this era of space flights it's not easy for a poet to keep up with the jargon, technological know-how, the parlance and the speed of the times, and yet the idiom of exploration and adventure is always appealing. There was some fun to be had in all this, along with a wry sense that astronauts command more interest than poets, and that among the small poetry audience, some poets command larger audiences than others. By this narrowing process, *elite* gets nearer and nearer to *eclipsed* as the process advances by refined gradations."

GERRIT HENRY was born in Baldwin, New York, in 1950, and graduated with a B.A. in English from Columbia University in 1972. His art criticism has appeared in *The New Republic, The New York Times,* and *Art in America*; he is a contributing editor of *Art News.* His monograph on the contemporary realist painter Janet Fish was published in 1987. His poems have appeared in *American Poetry Review, Poetry, Mudfish,* and other magazines.

Henry writes: "When I wrote 'The Confessions of Gerrit,' I thought of it as a kind of ironic lament. But audiences would laugh when I read the poem in public—*with* me, I trust, and not *at* me. On its own terms, the poem is very honest, which *can* be funny.

"The poem is in five stanzas of five lines each—it's a kind of overgrown ballad. Of course, I could have 'confessed' to far graver sins than I did. But this is poetry, and it's always good to hear people laugh."

JOHN HOLLANDER was born in New York City in 1929. He has published fifteen books of poetry, including *Spectral Emanations: New and Selected Poems* (Atheneum, 1978), *Powers of Thirteen* (Atheneum, 1983), and, most recently, *In Time and Place* (Johns Hopkins University Press, 1986). He is also the author of several books of criticism, such as *The Figure of Echo* (University of California Press, 1981), and coinventor with Anthony Hecht of the double dactyl, a light-verse form. He teaches at Yale University.

RICHARD HOWARD was born in Cleveland, Ohio, in 1929. He has published over 150 translations from the French, including Baudelaire's complete *Les Fleurs du mal* (Godine, 1982), for which he received the American Book Award for translation. In 1970 he was awarded the Pulitzer Prize for his third book of poems, *Untitled Subjects* (Atheneum, 1969). Subsequent collections include *Two-Part Inventions* (1974), *Misgivings* (1979), and *Lining Up* (1984), all published by Atheneum. His critical study of American poetry since 1950, *Alone with America* (Atheneum), was reissued in an expanded edition in 1980. He lives in New York City.

DONALD JUSTICE was born in Miami, Florida, in 1925. He teaches at the University of Florida. His first book, *The Summer Anniversaries* (Wesleyan University Press, 1960), was the Lamont Poetry Selection for 1959. It was followed by *Night Light* (Wesleyan University Press, 1967), *Departures* (Atheneum, 1973), and *Selected Poems* (Atheneum, 1979), which was awarded the Pulitzer Prize in 1980. He has also edited *The Collected Poems of Weldon Kees* (Stonewall, 1960). His latest book is *The Sunset Maker* (Atheneum, 1987).

Of "Nostalgia of the Lakefronts," Justice writes: "I had in mind Auden's 'Canzone' and the Dante on which it was modeled, but settled for something much simpler. The lake I thought of as like the Lake George of such painters as Kensett, Heade, and O'Keeffe, but my own childhood was spent a long way from any such demi-paradise. The childhood of the poem is entirely fictive. I would argue, nevertheless, that one is entitled to a certain nostalgia for what one never knew or had."

ROBERT KELLY teaches at Bard College and its Milton Avery Graduate School of the Arts. His latest collection of poems is *Not This Island Music* (Black Sparrow, 1987). He recently published his second book of short stories, *Doctor of Silence* (McPherson), and a long poem, *The Flowers of Unceasing Coincidence* (Station Hill Press, 1987).

Of "Hercules Musarum," Kelly writes: "I saw a small silver coin

that moved me, by image and text and object, all three. It was a
Roman denarius, of the mintmaster Pomponius Musa, and had been
minted in the late days of the Republic, 68–66 B.C. On the reverse
I saw in fine massy relief a form of Hercules I'd never heard of or
thought about. Naked, in the prime of life, facing right, the hero
holds a lyre. The sense is that he plays it, and by playing it could
lead the Muses as well as Apollo (shown on the observe) famously
does. Behind the lyre-player's back is an inscription: Hercules Mu-
sarum, Hercules of the Muses. The deity's title (*nomen numen*) may
only mean to flatter the mintmaster by a pun. But the coin itself
means: the naked body sings, and it is from the wield of body that
art comes.

"(My thanks to Linda Weintraub, curator of the Blum Gallery,
where I saw the coin in the exhibition 'Heracles,' devoted to the
transformations of Hercules in art. The coin is illustrated on plate
40 of Jaimee Pugliese Uhlenbrock, *Herakles* [New Rochelle, N.Y.:
Caratzas, 1986].)"

KEVIN KILLIAN was born on Long Island in 1952. He is the editor
of *Mirage* and the author of *Desiree* (1985). A story, "September,"
appears in *Men on Men: Best New Gay Fiction*, edited by George
Stambolian (New American Library, 1986). In April 1988 a play,
That, was performed by a cast of poets at Intersection Art Center
in San Francisco. He is married to the writer Dodie Bellamy; they
run the reading series at the bookstore Small Press Traffic and write
the review column "Signals" for its newsletter, *Traffic.* Killian is
writing a novel called *Shy* and a book of sex memoirs called *Bed-
rooms Have Windows.* He has lived in San Francisco since 1980.

Killian writes: "I wrote 'Pasolini' in the riddle form I associate
with Auden and Jack Spicer; at the same time I wrote a similar
poem that hasn't as yet found general acceptance, about the part in
Nastassia Kinski's hair. 'Pasolini' is kind of an 'answer' to Robert
Gluck's Pasolini poem (most easily found in his new book *Reader*
from Lapis Press), and I'd also been reading Kathy Acker's romance
My Death My Life by Pier Paolo Pasolini. My poem is part of a
longish, serial poem *Italy,* after Donald Britton's wonderful book
of the same title. Poetry doesn't 'connect,' Spicer said, it 'corre-
sponds.' "

AUGUST KLEINZAHLER was born in Jersey City, New Jersey, in 1949. He divides his time between New Jersey and the San Francisco Bay Area, where he has taught poetry at the University of California, Berkeley. He is the recipient of a General Electric Foundation Award for Younger Writers, and a collection of his poems, *Storm over Hackensack* (Moyer Bell, 1985), received the Bay Area Book Reviewers Award for poetry in 1985. "Soda Water with a Boyhood Friend" will appear in his forthcoming book, *Earthquake Weather,* to be published by Moyer Bell in spring 1989.

Kleinzahler writes: "When one chooses not to avert his eyes from the ordinary and its chief particulars, and then to pay attention, sometimes extraordinary vistas will suddenly everywhere abound."

CAROLINE KNOX graduated from Radcliffe College and from the University of Wisconsin, Milwaukee, with a Ph.D. in English in creative writing. Her collection *The House Party* was published by the University of Georgia Press in 1984. Her poems have appeared in *Poetry, Shenandoah, The American Scholar, The New Republic,* and elsewhere. She received a fellowship from the National Endowment for the Arts in 1986 and from the Ingram Merrill Foundation a year later. She lives in Westerly, Rhode Island, and teaches at the University of Connecticut, Avery Point.

Of "Movement Along the Frieze," Knox writes: "I'd wanted for a long time to write a poem on the subject of writing poetry, but attempts had turned out banal. So I decided to go at the problem obliquely, and make a sort of list poem containing some examples of problems and frustrations and pretentiousness we go through as writers. I teach composition as well as poetry writing, so I keep getting hit in the course of the day with comp terminology. So I wanted to put that into the poem. Also, I wanted to put in lots of elements that pretended to be specific but in fact weren't, so that the voice would be either complex or ambiguous. I was trying to give the poem some anxiety."

KENNETH KOCH was born in Cincinnati, Ohio, in 1925. He graduated from Harvard in 1948 and took a doctorate at Columbia eleven years later. His books of poetry include *Thank You* (Grove, 1962), *When the Sun Tries to Go On* (Black Sparrow, 1969), *The Pleasures of Peace* (Grove, 1969), *The Art of Love* (Random House, 1975), *The Burning Mystery of Anna in 1951* (Random House, 1979), and *Days and Nights* (Random House, 1982). He is the author of four books on education, including *Wishes, Lies and Dreams* (Vintage, 1971) and *Rose, Where Did You Get That Red?* (Random House, 1973). Koch's *Selected Poems, 1950–1982* was published in 1985 by Random House. Knopf published his *One Thousand Avant-Garde Plays* in 1988. He lives in New York City, where he is a professor of English at Columbia University.

Koch writes: "I like the uncompromising title of the anthology."

JOHN KOETHE was born in San Diego, California, on December 25, 1945. He was graduated from Princeton University in 1967 and received his Ph.D. in philosophy from Harvard in 1973. Currently he is an associate professor of philosophy at the University of Wisconsin, Milwaukee. His books of poetry include *Blue Vents* (1968), *Domes* (Columbia University Press, 1973), and *The Late Wisconsin Spring* (Princeton University Press, 1984). He received the 1973 Frank O'Hara Award (for *Domes*) and the 1986 Bernard F. Conners Prize from *The Paris Review* (for "Mistral"). A Guggenheim Fellow for 1987–88, he has published papers on the philosophy of language and metaphysics, as well as art and literary criticism.

Of "Mistral," Koethe writes: " 'Mistral' was orginally conceived as a much shorter poem in three parts, which kept stretching out as I wrote to join together the lines and fragments I'd started out with. Since most of my recent poems had been in the first person, I wanted to avoid that pronoun until the close of the poem. Instead, I decided to employ, in the second section, a fictional character (inspired by a photograph on the cover of a book that happened to be on the table). I found it liberating to express imaginary sentiments without worrying too much about whether they rang true to my own experience. Moreover, it provided an additional pretext for the poem itself, which is largely concerned with the character of fiction and the imagination. Prosodically, I wanted to explore the use of polysyllabic words and long, prosaic lines bound together by assonance. This is something I have continued to do, having just recently completed another poem ('The Constructor') almost as long as 'Mistral,' but with no stanza breaks whatsoever."

PHILIP LAMANTIA was born in San Francisco in 1927. After early association with surrealists-in-exile in New York City in the mid-1940s, he lived in Europe, North Africa, and Mexico. He is the author of nine books of poetry, the most recent of which are *Becoming Visible* (1981) and *Meadowlark West* (1985), both published by City Lights Books. Now living in California, he has a keen interest in birds, wilderness preservation, and other ecological issues.

ANN LAUTERBACH was born in New York City in 1942. From 1967 until 1974 she lived in London, where she worked as an editor at Thames and Hudson Publishers. Since her return to New York City, she has worked as the director of the Max Protetch Gallery, has written art criticism, and has taught in the M.F.A. programs at Columbia University, Brooklyn College, and the Writers' Workshop in Iowa. She is the recipient of a Guggenheim Fellowship (1967) and an Ingram Merrill Foundation Grant (1988). Her books of poetry include *Many Times, But Then* (University of Texas Press, 1979) and *Before Recollection* (Princeton University Press, 1987). She has been a contributing editor of *Conjunctions* magazine since 1982.

DAVID LEHMAN, the series editor of *The Best American Poetry*, was born in New York City in 1948. A book critic for *Newsweek* and a contributing editor of *Partisan Review*, he has received poetry fellowships from the National Endowment for the Arts and from the Ingram Merrill Foundation. *An Alternative to Speech*, his most recent collection of poems, was published by Princeton University Press in 1986. He is the editor of *Ecstatic Occasions, Expedient Forms,* an anthology comprising poems and commentary by sixty-five contemporary poets (Collier Books, 1988). He lives in Ithaca, New York, with his wife and son.

Of "Operation Memory," Lehman writes: "I've long been fascinated by military code names, such as Operation Torch for the Allied invasion of North Africa. 'Operation Memory' suggested a military metaphor for an autobiographical reflection. Or was memory (or its loss) a metaphor for a military experience? Perhaps both. I set out to write a poem about the war in Vietnam. (An undeclared war, Vietnam is nowhere mentioned in the poem.) 'Operation Memory' is a sestina with a variable. Ordinarily, there are six repeating end-words in a sestina. Here there are five fixed end-words and a sequence of numbers where the sixth would go. It's a downward progression (hundred, fifty, eighteen, ten, one) plus a year (1970) and an age (38, the age I was when I wrote the poem). I thought of Abraham trying to persuade God to spare the sinful cities: if there were fifty righteous men, would he do it? If there were twenty righteous men? Ten? I was recently asked whether the speaker commits suicide at the end of the poem ('a loaded gun on my lap'). That's one possibility; a second is that he is about to shoot somebody else; a third is that it's 'a loaded gun' in metaphor only."

PHILIP LEVINE was born in Detroit in 1928. "A Walk with Tom Jefferson" is the title poem of his new book, his thirteenth, which Knopf is publishing in 1988. Levine's work has won the National Book Critics Circle Award, the American Book Award, the Lenore Marshall Award, and most recently the Ruth Lilly Poetry Prize from *Poetry* magazine and the American Council for the Arts in recognition of outstanding poetic achievement. He lives in Fresno, California.

Of "A Walk with Tom Jefferson," Levine writes: "The poem was born out of a visit back to Detroit, the first city of my life. I had a long conversation with a man, a black man slightly younger than I, that supplied me with many of the insights and even much of the language of the poem. The 'neighborhood' of the poem is one I'd known very well as a young man, since I worked for a couple of years there."

NATHANIEL MACKEY was born in Miami, Florida, in 1947 and grew up in California. He is the author of two chapbooks of poetry, *Four for Trane* (Golemics, 1978) and *Septet for the End of Time* (Boneset, 1983), as well as a book of poetry, *Eroding Witness* (University of Illinois Press, 1985), which was selected for publication in the National Poetry Series. *Bedouin Hornbook,* the first volume of a work-in-progress titled *From a Broken Bottle Traces of Perfume Still Emanate,* was published in 1986 by the University of Kentucky Press in the Callaloo Fiction Series. He edits the literary magazine *Hambone* and teaches at the University of California, Santa Cruz.

MICHAEL MALINOWITZ was born in New York City in 1951. Educated at American University (B.A. in literature) and Brooklyn College (M.F.A. in creative writing), he is coeditor of *The Bad Henry Review,* a literary magazine. He is the vice president of a sales promotion organization. His poems have appeared in numerous magazines and in the anthology *Ecstatic Occasions, Expedient Forms* (Collier Books, 1988). He lives with his wife in Greenwich Village and goes to Florida for spring training every March.

Malinowitz writes: " 'Funeral March for a Papagallo' was written in a deliberate attempt to achieve what I consider a reductive quality or appearance that is usually not evident in my work. I hoped to transmute one of my father's businessman stories into a poem."

TOM MANDEL was born in Chicago in 1942 and attended the University of Chicago, doing graduate studies in the Committee on Social Thought, working with Hannah Arendt, Saul Bellow, and Harold Rosenberg. A poet and entrepreneur, Mandel lives in San Francisco. He has published *Ready to Go* (Ithaca House, 1981), *Erat* (Burning Deck, 1981), *Central Europe* (Coincidence Press, 1986), and *Some Appearances* (Jimmy's House of Knowledge, 1987). *Realism* is forthcoming from Burning Deck and *The Common Warfare* is under way.

HARRY MATHEWS was born in New York City in 1930. His most recent books are *Armenian Papers: Poems 1954–1984* (Princeton University Press, 1987) and *Cigarettes,* his fourth novel (Collier Books, 1988). His first two novels, *The Conversions* (Random House, 1962) and *Tlooth* (Doubleday, 1966), were recently reprinted in paperback by Carcanet Press. He divides his time between Paris and New York.

Mathews writes: "Written in 1982, 'Histoire' no doubt harks back to the enthusiastic and edgy days of the late '60s and early '70s when, more obviously than usual, sex and politics bubbled in a single pot."

BERNADETTE MAYER was born in 1945. She is the author of *Studying Hunger, Memory* (North Atlantic, 1975), *Midwinter Day* (Turtle Island Foundation, 1982), *Memory's Book of Hours, Mutual Aid,* and *Utopia* (United Artists, 1984). She is a contributor to *The Teachers & Writers Handbook of Poetic Forms* and coauthor, with Dale Worsley, of a new book on the teaching of science writing. Her new book is *Sonnets.* She lives in New York City.

Mayer writes: " 'Holding the Thought of Love' is a sonnet dedicated to a young poet and painter Bill DeNoyelles. One day we had traveled about the city, then took a walk in my neighborhood while photographing and conversing. Bill was upset by certain aspects of the ways of being poets and artists; we were both worried about living or life in the city. The sonnet form has always seemed appropriate to me for the solutions of problems, and so I wrote this poem."

JAMES MERRILL was born in New York City in 1926. He received his B.A. from Amherst in 1947 and published his *First Poems* (Knopf) in 1951. His subsequent books have won him two National Book Awards (for *Nights and Days* [1966] and *Mirabell* [1978]), the Bollingen Prize in poetry (for *Braving the Elements* [1972]), and the Pulitzer Prize (for *Divine Comedies* [1976]), all published by Atheneum. *From the First Nine: Poems 1946–1976* was published in 1983 by Atheneum with a companion volume, *The Changing Light at Sandover,* which includes the long narrative poem begun with "The Book of Ephraim" in *Divine Comedies* plus *Mirabell* and *Scripts for the Pageant* (Atheneum, 1980) in their entirety. *Sandover* received the National Book Critics Circle Award for 1983. Merrill's new book of poems, *The Inner Room,* will be published by Knopf in the fall of 1988. He divides his time between Stonington, Connecticut, and Key West, Florida.

EILEEN MYLES was born in Cambridge, Massachusetts, in 1949. From 1984 through 1986 she was artistic director of the Poetry Project at St. Mark's Church in New York City. Her books include *The Real Drive* (Semiotexte, forthcoming), *Bread and Water* (Hanuman, 1986), *Sappho's Boat* (Little Caesar, 1982), and *The Irony of the Leash* (1978). She teaches at New York University.

Of "Public Television," Myles writes: "The postpublication history of this poem is kind of odd. The day I saw it in *Shiny,* where it first appeared, I had only moments before bought *Mediations* by Martin Esslin at the St. Mark's Bookstore across the street. *Mediations* was the book that inspired the poem, I had read it at someone else's home, Zeborah's, she's the woman in the poem. I had been wanting the book for a couple of years—it's very interesting, it's about Max Reinhardt and Brecht and radio plays and everything I care about this year. The structuralism and the TV are still in there also, but I no longer care about those things. Anyhow, it all seemed terribly mystical at the time."

A. L. NIELSEN was born in Grand Island, Nebraska, and spent the better part of his life in Washington, D.C., before moving to San Jose, California, in 1987 to assume a position as assistant professor of English at San Jose State University. His first book of poetry, *Heat Strings,* was published by SOS Publications, and he has just published a scholarly examination of racism and poets titled *Reading Race* with the University of Georgia Press. He is the winner of the Larry Neal Award for poetry, the SAMLA Studies award for criticism, and grants from the DC Commission on the Arts and Humanities.

Nielsen writes: " 'Route E' is a selection from an unpublished long poem titled *Evacuation Routes: A User's Guide,* which juxtaposes language from disparate registers (nineteenth-century romance, twentieth-century dictionaries, the Yellow Pages, etc.) which seem to manifest the same obsessions. As the title implies, it is meant to be self-explanatory."

RON PADGETT was born in Tulsa, Oklahoma, in 1942. He received his B.A. from Columbia University in 1964. Since 1969 he has been associated with Teachers & Writers Collaborative and numerous Poets in the Schools programs in New York City. His books include *Triangles in the Afternoon* (SUN, 1980), *Toujours l'amour* (SUN, 1976), *Tulsa Kid* (Z Press, 1980), and *Great Balls of Fire* (Holt, 1969; revised edition forthcoming from SUN), as well as a translation of Guillaume Apollinaire, *The Poet Assassinated and Other Stories* (North Point, 1984). He is the editor of *The Complete*

Poems of Edwin Denby (Random House, 1986) and *The Teachers &
Writers Handbook of Poetic Forms* (Teachers & Writers Collaborative,
1987). "Light As Air" will be issued with etchings by Alex Katz.

MICHAEL PALMER was born in New York City in 1943. He has lived
in San Francisco since 1969. His books include *Blake's Newton* (1972),
The Circular Gates (1974), and *Without Music* (1977), all from Black
Sparrow Press, and *Notes for Echo Lake* (1981) and *First Figure* (1984)
from North Point Press. His new book, *Sun*, will be published in
the fall of 1988. Palmer has edited a collection of writings on poetics,
Code of Signals (North Atlantic, 1983), and has collaborated on a
number of dance works with Margaret Jenkins and the members
of her company. He is currently visiting professor of writing at the
University of California, Berkeley.

Of "From C," Palmer writes: "In the context of my other work,
'From C' stands as a point of necessary reduction or loss. It represents
an arrival, perhaps also an erotics of silence. And an eroteme? It is
mirrored by another sequence of the same length, also called 'C'."

BOB PERELMAN was born in Youngstown, Ohio, in 1947. He is the
author of eight books of poems, most recently *The First World* (The
Figures, 1986) and *Face Value* (Roof Press). His next book, *Captive
Audience*, is forthcoming from The Figures. He is also the editor
of *Writing/Talks* (1985), an anthology of talks by writers, published
by Southern Illinois University Press. He lives in Berkeley, Cali-
fornia, with his wife and two children.

Perelman writes: "It's no more possible to escape politics than it
is to escape economics. But to a reader who doesn't know my
work, the poem 'Politics' may not look that *political*—there's no
issue-oriented exhortation or analysis. However, what does occur
here as well as elsewhere in my work is a critique of the split
between daily experience and language. A short synopsis of this
critique might run as follows: we live in a social environment that
rings with administered rhetoric—from State of the Union ad-
dresses down to the assurance of quality on my tube of toothpaste
signed 'Your friend, Tom.' Political and commercial figures address
an atomized public of voters or consumers with ever more personal
immediacy. In 'Politics' this seems to translate into hospitals, cars,

posters speaking with confidence to a more ambiguous, troubled group: 'people'—either 'I,' 'you,' or 'we' for whom secure meaning now exists only somewhere else, in the past, in the Middle Ages, in dreams, in a script, and whose present is very unstable, with hardware stores being replaced by jogging stores and the televised pleasure offered by BMW ads hard to tell apart from being in an ambulance.''

ROBERT PINSKY was born in Long Branch, New Jersey, in 1940. He has published three books of poetry: *Sadness and Happiness* (1975), *An Explanation of America* (1979), both from Princeton University Press, and, most recently, *History of My Heart* (Ecco, 1984). He is also the author of an interactive computer novel, *Mindwheel* (Broderbund, San Rafael, Calif.). A collection of his essays, *Poetry and the World*, is forthcoming in 1988 from Ecco Press.

DONALD REVELL teaches at the University of Denver. His first collection, *From the Abandoned Cities*, was published by Harper & Row in 1983; his second, *The Gaza of Winter*, appeared in spring 1988 from the University of Georgia Press.

Revell writes: " 'St. Lucy's Day,' from a new manuscript in progress, is probably the title poem of that manuscript. The circumstances around my composition of the poem were dual: one being my long admiration for Donne's 'Nocturnall upon St. Lucie's Day,' the second being the yearly party I give on that day (December 13). Both poem and party have always made me feel called upon to examine myself and my current motives more rigorously than I usually do, perhaps because both make me feel suspended between absolute light and absolute darkness, between my affection for the present and its possible futures on the one hand, and my hopeless devotion to the clutter of my private past on the other.''

JOE ROSS was born in 1960. *Guards of the Heart,* his first book, is a collection of four of his poetic plays (forthcoming from Sun & Moon Press). He lives in Washington, D.C.

Ross writes: "True art falls away—revealing the nearly secret source from which it came—Where someone was allowed to reach—struggle—and give it birth—To bring to light in a near perfect reflection—a swiftly still moment—A moment that absolutely mirrors oneself, one's other, the world—and still speaks—has something definite to say.

"Read—absorb—allow the borders to be crossed—Step past the boundaries—those walls which we put up—put up with.

"Participate—true art is large enough to contain you—Large enough to overcome even the distinction of you and the work as separate—Not an adding of one to another—nor subtraction—rather an entering in—into a world where the walls break & we are allowed peace—a place—home."

LESLIE SCALAPINO, born in 1948, is the publisher of O Books. Her books of poetry include *Considering how exaggerated music is* (1982), *that they were at the beach* (1985), and *way* (1988), all published by North Point Press. She lives in Oakland, California.

JAMES SCHUYLER was born in Chicago in 1923. His books of poetry include *Freely Espousing* (Doubleday, 1969), *The Crystal Lithium* (Random House, 1972), *Hymn to Life* (Random House, 1974), *The Morning of the Poem* (Farrar, Straus & Giroux, 1980), and *A Few Days* (Random House, 1985). *The Morning of the Poem* won the Pulitzer Prize. He has also published three novels, one of them written in collaboration with John Ashbery. James Schuyler's *Selected Poems* was published in 1988 by Farrar, Straus & Giroux. He lives in New York City.

Schuyler writes: "Among the poems I've written since mid-'85 there are several about entertainers (Duke Ellington, Mildred Bailey, Brook Benton, Simone Signoret), but it wasn't a plan, or even new: 'Beautiful Funerals,' about Libby Holman & a lot of others, was written in '71."

DAVID SHAPIRO was born in Newark, New Jersey, in 1947. He studied at Clare College, Cambridge, on a Kellett Fellowship for two years following his graduation from Columbia University in 1968. His books of poetry include *January* (Holt, 1965), *Poems from Deal* (Dutton, 1969), *A Man Holding an Acoustic Panel* (Dutton, 1971), *The Page-Turner* (Liveright, 1973), *Lateness* (Overlook Press, 1977), *To an Idea* (Overlook, 1983), and the forthcoming *House*

(Blown Apart). He has published a critical study of John Ashbery's poetry as well as monographs on the painters Jim Dine and Jasper Johns. The recipient of fellowships from both the National Endowment for the Arts and the National Endowment for the Humanities, he is currently associate professor in art history at William Paterson College in Wayne, New Jersey. He lives in New York City with his wife and son.

Of "Empathy for David Winfield," Shapiro writes: "Consultant for an exhibition on baseball, I had no poems in which baseball was the center, though the stadium appeared obliquely in many poems. It is said baseball is the only metaphysical sport, since it need never end. Marianne Moore, a fan of baseball, once wrote when I was seventeen that my poetry was not stark enough but she too lacked dynamite. Brooding on adequate starkness, on her revision of 'Poetry,' I have reduced a longer poem of mine, 'To the Earth,' to my Last Poem: 'I fell with my father through space / Madly in love with the earth.' To those who find the sports poem too whimsical, I can only offer that as my epitaph and the remark of my friendly critic Jeremy Gilbert-Rolfe, who says that art is not a game. Nor is poetry our dreams, but we may employ them. My favorite medium: eraser fluid. (A favored Russian definition of poetry: 'The articulatory dance of the speech-organs.')"

CHARLES SIMIC was born in Yugoslavia in 1938. Educated at New York University, he teaches at the University of New Hampshire. In 1983 he received a MacArthur Foundation Fellowship. His eleventh and twelfth books of poems are *Selected Poems 1963–1983* (Braziller, 1985) and *Unending Blues* (Harcourt Brace Jovanovich, 1986). He is married and the father of two children.

Of "St. Thomas Aquinas," Simic writes: "When I left Chicago in 1958, to move to New York, I took with me Dante's *Divine Comedy* and a collection of Aquinas's writing. I had read Dante before, and Aquinas was supposed to explain Dante. I lost Dante on the train, and Aquinas I read during those first, penniless months in New York."

GARY SNYDER was born in San Francisco in 1930. At Reed College in Portland, Oregon, he did an interdepartmental major in literature and anthropology, B. A., 1951. In 1956 he went to Kyoto, Japan, to pursue studies in Far Eastern culture and Zen Buddhist texts. The Japan years lasted through 1968. Since 1970, he has been living in the northern Sierra Nevada on the edge of the Tahoe National Forest. He has been a member of the English department of the University of California, Davis, since 1985. Snyder has published fourteen books of poetry and prose. *Turtle Island* (New Directions, 1974) won the Pultizer Prize for poetry in 1975.

Of "Walking the New York Bedrock," Snyder writes: "I found myself walking through the streets of Manhattan one week in May, feeling it to be as thoroughly natural as any wilderness, and perceiving it with my ears, and the back of my neck. The poem was composed over five days."

RUTH STONE received a Whiting Writer's Award in 1986. Her most recent book of poems, *Second Hand Coat*, was published by David Godine in 1987. She lives in Vermont.

MAY SWENSON was born in Logan, Utah. Her books of poetry include *A Cage of Spines* (Rinehart, 1958), *To Mix with Time: New and Selected Poems* (Scribner's, 1963), *Half Sun Half Sleep* (Scribner's, 1967), *New and Selected Things Taking Place* (Little Brown, 1978), and *In Other Words* (Knopf, 1987). She translated from the Swedish the selected poems of Tomas Tranströmer, *Windows and Stones* (University of Pittsburgh Press, 1972). She has received, among other honors and awards, Rockefeller and Guggenheim grants, a Ford Foundation grant, the Bollingen Prize in poetry and, most recently, a MacArthur Fellowship.

Of "Dummy, 51, to Go to Museum. Ventriloquist Dead at 75," Swenson writes: "The title of the poem is exactly that of the headline over the news item."

JAMES TATE was born in Kansas City, Missouri, in 1943. He was awarded the Yale Younger Poets prize in 1966. His most recent books of poetry are *Constant Defender* (Ecco, 1983) and *Reckoner* (Wesleyan University Press, 1986). He teaches at the University of Massachusetts.

LYDIA TOMKIW was born in 1959 in Chicago, where she has been a lifelong resident. She holds a B.A. in Writing / English and an M.A. in Inter-Arts Education from Columbia College in Chicago. Her recent poetry collections include *Violins* (Center Press) and *Big Skin* (Buzzerama); her fifth collection is forthcoming from Wide Skirt Press in England. She is currently collaborating with her husband, Don Hedeker; under the name Algebra Suicide, they have released five recorded collections of poetry and music.

Tomkiw writes: "When working with palindromes (words, phrases, sentences that read the same backward as forward), you get a good sense of how content can be at the mercy of form. There's little room to toy with the placement of words, and their proximity to each other often threatens implosion. But language is so awesome and flexible: it can reinvent itself, and force content through any constraint imposed on it.

"Each line of 'Six of Ox Is' is a palindrome—but I know people who understand the poem without realizing that."

DEREK WALCOTT was born in St. Lucia, the West Indies, in 1930, and now lives in Trinidad and Boston. His books of poetry include *Another Life* (Three Continents, 1982), *The Star-Apple Kingdom* (1979), *The Fortunate Traveller* (1982), *Midsummer* (1984), and, most recently, *The Arkansas Testament* (1987), all four published by Farrar, Straus & Giroux. He has also published a number of plays, including *The Joker of Seville and O Babylon!* (1978) and *Remembrance and Pantomime* (1980), both from Farrar, Straus & Giroux.

ROSANNE WASSERMAN was born in Kentucky in 1952. She declared a major in poetry and poetics at Indiana University and took an M.F.A. from Columbia University, then a doctorate from the City University of New York Graduate Center. She has worked as an editor at the Metropolitan Museum of Art and as a teacher in New York City grade schools, high schools, and colleges. She is married to the poet Eugene D. Richie.

Wasserman writes: "I wrote 'Inuit and Seal' in Montreal, while visiting the writer Gaëtan Racine. He was living then in an old house, its back porch full of flowers and vines. His friend Jim, who renovated the building, worked in the north with Inuit tribes. They had given him a stone sculpture: a crouching hunter, lifting a wooden spear above a perfectly circular hole in a thin stone slab. Under the slab, curved around the base of the sculpture, a giant seal swam right up to the hole. That weekend, almost everyone in Montreal got dressed up all in pink, for a rock concert called 'La Vie en Rose.' "

MARJORIE WELISH was born in New York City in 1944. She is the author of *Handwritten* (SUN, 1979) and a chapbook, *Two Poems* (Z Press, 1981). Her poems are anthologized in *Ecstatic Occasions, Expedient Forms*, edited by David Lehman (Collier Books, 1988), and *Up Late*, edited by Andrei Codrescu (Four Walls Eight Windows, 1987). She has worked as an art critic for the past twenty years.

Welish writes: " 'Respected, Feared, and Somehow Loved' emerged in response to a rereading of *The Iliad*, and more specifically, from my attempt, after a day's immersion in the text, to characterize the litigation going on among the gods on behalf of the heroes warring on earth. This germ of content was all I needed to begin the poem, since I had already chosen the form: a lyric created by lines proceeding in repetition or leaps, but in any event, installing sense through the extremities of similarity and difference. By these means, a kind of mania invaded the lyric, suitable for expressing the mortal enterprise of life conducted on a grand scale."

SUSAN WHEELER was born in Pittsburgh in 1955. Her poems have appeared in *Sulfur, Shenandoah, Massachusetts Review*, and other magazines. In 1987 she received the Grolier Award. She lives in New York City.

Of "What Memory Reveals," Wheeler writes: "I had imagined this as a kind of generic biography, which would apply to almost anyone I know."

RICHARD WILBUR was born in New York City in 1921. World War II took him to Cassino, Anzio, and the Siegfried Line. After the war he earned an M.A. at Harvard, spent three years at the university's Society of Fellows, then taught at Harvard, Wellesley, and Wesleyan. He has translated Molière's *The Misanthrope* and *Tartuffe* and Racine's *Phedre*. His books of poetry include *The Beautiful*

Changes (Reynal & Hitchcock, 1947), *Ceremony* (1950), *Things of This World* (1956), *Advice to a Prophet* (1961), and *Walking to Sleep* (1969), all from Harcourt Brace Jovanovich, and *Digging for China* (Doubleday, 1970). Harcourt Brace Jovanovich is publishing his *New and Collected Poems* in 1988. Wilbur, who divides his time between Cummington, Massachusetts, and Key West, Florida, succeeded Robert Penn Warren as the nation's second official poet laureate.

Of "Trolling for Blues," Wilbur writes: "John Hersey, when he was beginning to write his book *Blues,* asked me if I had a poem about fish or fishing which he could incorporate into the text. If not, he said, why not write one? It turned out that I wanted to write a poem about fish—indeed, about bluefish; but I worked slowly, as usual, and Hersey's book went to press before my last stanza had jelled. Fortunately, my poem could be slipped into the book at the time of the fifth printing."

ALAN WILLIAMSON was born in Chicago in 1944. He teaches at the University of California at Davis, and lives in Albany, California. He has published two collections of poems, *Presence* (1983) and *The Muse of Distance* (1988), both from Knopf. He has also published two books of criticism, including *Pity the Monsters: The Political Vision of Robert Lowell* (Yale University Press, 1974).

Williamson writes: "With 'Recitation,' I wanted to write a political poem that might actually help, by enabling people to imagine that we could dismantle our arsenals, and could live with the knowledge that, until the end of time, we would have to choose not to rebuild and use them. Some negative rules immediately set themselves, out of my dislike of most antinuclear poems: no presumptuous descriptions of Hiroshima; no denunciations of public figures, ignoring our collective complicity in what the late Terrence Des Pres called 'the nuclear sublime'; no easy dismissal of 'civilization' per se. Once I rejected these facile resources, I found others flocking to me from the culture at large: not only obvious ones like the ABC-TV movie *The Day After* and Jonathan Schell's *The Fate of the Earth,* but Bach's St. Matthew Passion, the 'death of God' theologians, the experiences of someone close to me in a chronic-pain program in Boston. All of this somehow helped me in imagining and imaging a way out."

JOHN YAU, writer and critic, was born in Lynn, Massachusetts, in 1950. He is the author of numerous books of poetry as well as monographs, essays, and reviews. Among his recent collections are *Cenotaph* (1988), *Corpse and Mirror* (Holt Rinehart & Winston, 1983), and *Broken Off by the Music* (Burning Deck, 1981). Since 1978, he has written for *Art in America, Artforum, Flash Art, Parkett, Art News,* and *SF Camerawork,* among other magazines. He is a contributing editor of *Sulfur* and is currently on the graduate faculty of Pratt Institute in Brooklyn, New York, and the Milton Avery Graduate School of the Arts (Bard College). He has received fellowships from the Ingram Merrill Foundation and the National Endowment for the Arts.

GEOFFREY YOUNG was born in Los Angeles in 1944. He lives in Great Barrington, Massachusetts, where he edits and publishes *The Figures,* a string of new poetry books. " 'Drive, It Said' was written in the winter of 1986–87, taking its initial impulse from a dream he had in which he was playing 'Like Someone in Love' on cornet. The breakup of his marriage, life lived alone and apart from family, a small rented house dubbed The Blue Lagoon, transitional angst. Stories began to attach themselves to the narrative, recollections from an earlier adventurous time alone in Europe. Whether called love, pain, or grief, the only response is to feel it, allow it to sensitize the language, and keep moving." The author of *Rocks and Deals, Subject to Fits,* and *Elegies,* Young teaches in the writing department of Columbia University in New York City.

MAGAZINES WHERE THE POEMS
WERE FIRST PUBLISHED

Aerial, ed. Rod Smith. P.O. Box 25642, Washington, D.C. 20007

American Poetry Review, ed. David Bonanno, Stephen Berg, and Arthur Vogelsang. Temple University Center City, 1616 Walnut Street, Room 405, Philadelphia, Pa. 19103

Antaeus, ed. Daniel Halpern. The Ecco Press, 26 West 17th Street, N.Y. 10011

Boulevard, ed. Richard Burgin. 2400 Chestnut Street, #3301, Philadelphia, Pa. 19103

Conjunctions, ed. Bradford Morrow. 33 West 9th Street, New York, N.Y. 10011

Epoch, ed. Cecil Giscombe. 251 Goldwin Smith Hall, Cornell University, Ithaca, N.Y. 14853

Exquisite Corpse, ed. Andrei Codrescu. Culture Shock Foundation, English Department, Louisiana State University, Baton Rouge, La. 70803

Grand Street, ed. Ben Sonnenberg. 50 Riverside Drive, New York, N.Y. 10024

The Hudson Review, ed. Paula Deitz and Frederick Morgan. 684 Park Avenue, New York, N.Y. 10021

Mudfish, ed. Jill Hoffman and Jill Gallen. Box Turtle Press/Attitude Art, Inc. 184 Franklin Street, New York, N.Y. 10013

New American Writing, ed. Maxine Chernoff and Paul Hoover. 2920 West Pratt, Chicago, Ill. 60645

The New Republic, poetry ed. Richard Howard. 1220 19th Street, NW, Washington, D.C. 20036

The New Yorker, poetry ed. Alice Quinn. 25 West 43rd Street, New York, N.Y. 10036

O.blēk, ed. Peter Gizzi and Connell McGrath. Box 836, Stockbridge, Mass. 01262

The Paris Review, poetry ed. Patricia Storace. 541 East 72nd Street, New York, N.Y. 10021

Partisan Review, ed. William Phillips. Boston University, 141 Bay State Road, Boston, Mass. 02215

Poetry, ed. Joseph Parisi. 60 West Walton Street, Chicago, Ill. 60610

Shenandoah, ed. James Boatwright. The Washington and Lee University Review, Box 722, Lexington, Va. 24450

Shiny International, ed. Steven Hall. 129 Second Avenue, Suite 17, New York, N.Y. 10003

Sonora Review. Department of English, University of Arizona, Tuscon, Ariz. 85721

Sulfur, ed. Clayton Eshleman. English Department, Eastern Michigan University, Ypsilanti, Mich. 48197

Tyuonyi, ed. Phillip Foss. Institute of American Indian Arts, St. Michael Drive, Santa Fe, N.M. 87501

Verse, ed. Henry Hart. Department of English, College of William and Mary, Williamsburg, Va. 23185

The Yale Review, poetry ed. J. D. McClatchy. P. O. Box 1902A Yale Station, New Haven, Conn. 06520

ACKNOWLEDGMENTS

Grateful acknowledgment is made to the publications from which the poems in this volume were chosen. Unless specifically noted otherwise, copyright of the poems is held by the individual poets.

A. R. Ammons: "Motion Which Disestablishes Organizes Everything" is reprinted by permission from *The Hudson Review*, vol. XL, no. 2, Summer 1987. Copyright © 1987 by The Hudson Review, Inc.

Ralph Angel: "Shadow Play" appeared originally in *Poetry*, January 1987. Copyright © 1987 by The Modern Poetry Association. Reprinted by permission of the poet and the editor of *Poetry*.

Rae Armantrout: "Bases" appeared originally in *O.blēk*, #2, 1987. Reprinted by permission.

John Ash: "Memories of Italy" is reprinted from *Disbelief* by John Ash (Carcanet, 1987). Copyright © 1987 by John Ash. Reprinted with permission of Carcanet Press, New York.

John Ashbery: "One Coat of Paint" appeared originally in *Shenandoah*, vol. 37, no. 3, 1987, and in *April Galleons* by John Ashbery (Viking, 1987). All rights reserved. Reprinted by permission of Viking Penguin Inc.

Ted Berrigan: "My Autobiography" appeared in *New American Writing*, #2, 1987. Reprinted by permission of the editors and of Alice Notley.

Mei-mei Berssenbrugge: "Chinese Space" appeared originally in *Conjunctions*, #10, 1987. Reprinted by permission.

George Bradley: "*Noch Einmal, an Orpheus*" appeared originally in *Grand Street*, Autumn 1987. Reprinted by permission.

Stefan Brecht: "Momentariness" appeared originally in *Tyuonyi*, # 3, 1987. Reprinted by permission.

Joseph Brodsky: "To Urania" appeared originally in *The Paris Review*, Summer 1987, and in *To Urania* by Joseph Brodsky. Reprinted by permission of Farrar, Straus & Giroux, Inc.

Nicholas Christopher: "Miranda in Reno" appeared originally in *The New Republic*, January 26, 1987. Reprinted by permission.

Marc Cohen: "Mecox Road" appeared originally in *Verse*, vol. 4, no. 2, 1987. Reprinted by permission.

Wanda Coleman: "Essay on Language" is reprinted from *Heavy Daughter Blues* by Wanda Coleman with the permission of Black Sparrow Press, 24 Tenth Street, Santa Rosa, Calif. 95401.

Clark Coolidge: "A Monologue" appeared originally in *O.blēk*, #2, 1987. Reprinted by permission.

Alfred Corn: "New York" appeared originally in *Partisan Review, #4,*